Many are cold and a few are frozen

A. J. Raitt takes a sideways look at the Christian life

Introduction by Bob Prouty

First published 2003
Copyright © 2003

All rights reserved. No part of this publication may be reproduced in any form without prior permission from the publisher.

British Library Cataloguing in Publication Data.
A catalogue record for this book is available from the British Library.

ISBN: 1-903921-07-4

Published by
Autumn House, Grantham, Lincs.
Printed in Thailand

Editor's Note

The items in this book first appeared as a popular column written by A. J. Raitt over a period of ten years in the fortnightly magazine *Messenger*. The selection of the items was made by Barrymore Bell. Since the manuscript was prepared A. J. Raitt has gone to his rest. He was a very wise, perceptive and warm person with a tremendous sense of humour. He was a Bible and Language teacher, and a church leader, for sixty years. He approved the selection from his magazine column 'Our Life Together' and Bob Prouty's Introduction prior to his last illness. A. J. Raitt's children, Margaret Raitt, Joan Maxwell and Lincoln Raitt, have given their permission for the publication of this book. In memory of their father, they have stipulated that all royalties be used to assist children to receive a Christian education at the Dudley House School.

Preface

Our Life Together: A sideways look at your congregation

'I gave him a piece of my mind,' 'I can only take so much,' 'Somebody ought to tell her,' 'I don't care what anybody says,' 'I can give as good as I get' – after a lifetime of careful listening in a caring pastoral and teaching ministry, A. J. Raitt uses the clichés he has overheard to make us think again about our approach to living at peace in a Christian congregation geared to mission.

> 'To dwell above with the saints in love –
> That will be glory!
> To dwell below with the saints I know –
> That's another story.'

This is a book about 'dwelling below' in the typical Christian congregation with all its faults and frailties and morphology of members. It was the author's contention that as we learn to live in harmony here, accepting God's grace to live graciously, we are practising to be participants in the great congregation in the Kingdom of Glory.

David Marshall, Editor

Introduction
by Bob Prouty

A CHURCHGOER'S BIRD GUIDE

Straightlaced Nitpicker

Closely related to the vulture family, the Straightlaced Nitpicker is noted for its ability to spot flaws from a great distance. It is handicapped, however, by monochromatic vision and sees everything only in black and white. The Nitpicker is easily recognised by the beam in its eye.

Jaded Pewwarmer

This common bird is easily spotted by the knowledgeable bird-watcher, but has a limited range of habitat. Likewise, it can be observed only at special times. It is almost never found at prayer meeting or in the front of the church, but can frequently be seen moving in vast numbers to the car park during communion services and altar calls.

Teenaged Twitterpate

The presence of the Teenaged Twitterpate is readily detected by its colourful plumage and more or less constant twittering. Both the plumage and the twittering are a part of an elaborate 'courtship' ritual which sometimes takes years. The twittering is especially apparent where Teenaged Twitterpates sit in pairs. The Twitterpate population has been steadily declining of late in certain churches, partly because of the ravages of the Straightlaced Nitpicker (see above). Great caution should be exercised in identifying the Teenaged Twitterpate, as it is frequently mistaken for the Jaded Pewwarmer, which it resembles at times but from which it is entirely distinct.

Underrated Dunnet and Glory-seeker Sezzleduitt

The Underrated Dunnet is an inconspicuous bird often overlooked, particularly in the range of its more colourful cousin, the Glory-seeker Sezzleduitt. The two species can be observed in conjunction with each other, however, if the habits of each are properly understood. In almost any area where a work project is under way, the astute bird-watcher will find a Glory-seeker Sezzleduitt, but if he checks again after the work is done, he'll find another Dunnet.

Duck-billed Platitude

Immediately recognisable by its call, which is high-sounding but with a hollow ring to it, the Duck-billed Platitude is not a true bird but is frequently found in association with Nitpickers and Pewwarmers. It also occurs commonly in sermons and is the natural prey of the Teenaged Twitterpate.

Naysaying Headshaker

The Naysaying Headshaker is a familiar sight at committee meetings and in church foyers. It is identifiable chiefly from its habit of moving its head emphatically back and forth and from its call, a loud CAN'T CAN'T CAN'T! repeated at regular intervals throughout the day. Its work habits closely resemble those of the Gloryseeker Sezzleduitt.

Everlasting Lovebird

A well-known Guidebook describes the general characteristics of the Everlasting Lovebird as follows: Love, joy, peace, long-suffering, gentleness, goodness, faith, meekness, temperance. Since the species does not occur naturally, each Lovebird must be individually produced and perfected over the years. A more exact description is difficult to give, *since Everlasting Lovebirds have been successfully developed from each of the species listed above* and since considerable variation exists at

A Churchgoer's Bird Guide

each stage of development. It should be noted further that the Creator of this remarkable process has himself been described variously as a dove, a mother hen, and as an eagle caring for its young.

Prouty's Point: Many readers will, of course, be able to recognise themselves in one or several of the above descriptions. Should any reader be unable to do so, succeeding rather in identifying most of his friends, he is advised to consult a more comprehensive bird guide for a full description of the Finger-pointing Namecaller.

And even if readers do not recognise themselves in any of the species given above, or as Finger-pointing Namecallers, they will certainly recognise themselves in A. J. Raitt's sideways look at church life. . . .

'A Churchgoer's Bird Guide' by Bob Prouty was first published in *Insight* magazine published by Review and Herald in the USA for young Christians.

'I gave her a piece of my mind'

There was no doubt about it; the girl's conduct had been reprehensible. Mrs Jones's face flushed with indignation as she recounted the incident. Then she declared in a voice of deep satisfaction, 'I gave her a piece of my mind.'

Now there are gifts and gifts, but there are some gifts one cannot afford to bestow. A piece of one's mind, for instance. It's rather on a par with Shylock's demand for his pound of flesh, which could not be obtained without the shedding of blood, and *that* he had not taken into his calculations. Giving others a piece of one's mind usually leaves the giver the poorer, apart from the fact that most of us haven't so much that we can afford to give any of it away. In fact, most people who indulge frequently in such gifts usually end up the poorer in spirituality and friendships. The momentary satisfaction at having given vent to our feelings frequently results in a nagging conscience which tells us that we said more than we intended to say. Once the tap is turned on we find it hard to stop the flow of words. We warm up to the subject and, in so doing, drive the wedge deeper and deeper between ourselves and the recipients of our assumed wisdom. Mind you, there is a time for straight talking, but it must be under control, or with the piece of mind will go our *peace* of mind and we shall find ourselves impoverished spiritually.

What we need to ask ourselves under such circumstances is whether what we are giving is really contributing something worthwhile to the other person or if we are merely trying to carry out a surgical operation – that of cutting the other down to size. The scalpel needs to be handled with care. I've read enough about surgery to know that more than one death has resulted from a surgeon's lack of skill or his clumsiness. And a surgeon has been trained for his task. We look with extreme disfavour on the charlatan. Perhaps we should pause to ask ourselves whether we are qualified for such a delicate task as trying to cure others' defects. Wounds of the spirit can be far more deadly than those resulting from the misuse of surgical implements. The latter can result in physical loss without eternal consequences, but that may not be true of clumsiness in dealing with the minds of men and women.

It is really a question of motive. When I express myself, is it for my personal satisfaction, a kind of safety valve for built-up pressures within, or is it truly a carefully-thought-out effort to contribute something to another's well-being?

'I can only take so much'

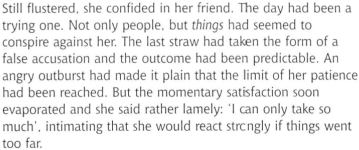

Still flustered, she confided in her friend. The day had been a trying one. Not only people, but *things* had seemed to conspire against her. The last straw had taken the form of a false accusation and the outcome had been predictable. An angry outburst had made it plain that the limit of her patience had been reached. But the momentary satisfaction soon evaporated and she said rather lamely: 'I can only take so much', intimating that she would react strongly if things went too far.

Now undoubtedly not only her friend heard her statement, but some imp reported her words to headquarters and immediately a plan of campaign was agreed upon. Said the devil, 'You now know exactly what to do. Make sure you provide all the irritations to bring her to her acknowledged breaking point, and she will be ours.'

It is a pity when we play into Satan's hands by telling him just what he has to do to get the better of us. Generals do not declare their weak points to the enemy. Neither should we to our foe who is out to take advantage of us at every opportunity.

Fortunately we have a Referee who will not allow our opponent to get an unfair advantage over us. He stands between us and our foe and says to us, 'I will not suffer you to be tempted above what you are able.' Consequently when a temptation comes to us we can say to ourselves, 'God has confidence that I can meet the foe on this point and be victorious.' Undoubtedly we shall gradually develop spiritual muscle and God will allow us to face sterner struggles, but never without providing a way out for us.

Let us, then, always bear these two things in mind: First, not to play into the enemy's hands by telling him that beyond a certain point he will gain the victory; and, second, if a challenge comes to us, it is because God knows we can not only meet it but be 'more than conquerors'. (Romans 8:37.)

'Never!'

'Never, never, never, and that's final!' There's not much good entering into an argument when such a categorical statement has been hurled at one. Silence or a change of subject is called for. But that little word 'never' needs careful handling. It places its user in a difficult situation. Take for example such expressions as: 'I'll never trust him again'; 'I never want to see her again'; 'I'll never speak to him again'. While they express passing annoyance, frustration or disapproval and so provide a kind of safety valve for pent-up emotions, by their very wording they also put shackles on one's relationships which the passing of time and change of circumstances may cause one to regret.

The truth is that life is not static. There are too many imponderables for it to be safe to declare what tomorrow's circumstances may require. And, 'never' includes an awful lot of 'tomorrows'.

Let's begin with ourselves. Not physically, mentally or spiritually do we want to be set as in a cast-iron mould.

'Never!'

Perhaps physically we would wish to remain as we are, if we are now in superlative form and health. But we know that that cannot be.

Confronted by the scriptural injunction to 'grow in grace and knowledge' (2 Peter 3:18), we cannot contemplate other than with alarm cessation of mental and spiritual development. And with development comes a casting off of the old and a putting on of the new; so that former limitations and impossibilities give way to greater achievements and deeper insights. Thus the 'me' of yesterday is no longer the 'me' of today; nor the 'me' of today the 'me' of tomorrow.

What is true of us is true also of the one with whom we have declared we never want to have further dealings. So while we ask God to accept the new 'me' brought about by his grace, we welcome the privilege of association with the new person his grace has created.

Is 'never' always to be avoided? By no means. When rightly used it is a word which Satan does his best to take from us. He would much rather have us say, 'I'll try anything once', for he knows that that first step is in many cases all that is needed to start us on the road to ruin. A resounding 'no' to his allurements, backed by a 'never', is the appropriate response. In that decision we are backed by a most important 'never', one we should never forget! It is reported in the epistle to the Hebrews chapter 13 verse 5, that Jesus promised, 'I will never leave thee, nor forsake thee.' That meets our present needs. But what of the future, the near future? We have the promise of citizenship in a kingdom 'which shall never be destroyed'. (Daniel 2:44.)

'Somebody ought to tell her!'

The concern in her voice was genuine. You could tell that there was no malice in what she said. It seemed a shame that someone she esteemed should be opening herself to adverse comment by some inconsistency of which she was apparently unaware. 'Somebody ought to tell her!' she exclaimed. Her friend asked: 'Why don't you?' 'What, me? I couldn't do that,' she replied. Then followed a string of reasons why it would be inappropriate for her to do so. But 'somebody' ought to.

Somebody is a very convenient person to have around. Many a distasteful or embarrassing task can be shifted on to his shoulders. Having been the chosen 'somebody' at times, I can understand another's wanting to pass on the responsibility. And it is often done with disarming expressions of confidence. 'You have had more experience! You can express yourself better. I get all tongue-tied and end up saying the wrong thing. You do it.'

There are those who rush in where angels fear to tread. They pride themselves on their forthrightness. The word 'tact' is not in their vocabulary. They have no hesitation in assuming a role which others would fill with the utmost reluctance. The results of their efforts can be painful to all concerned.

Both the readiness to rely on 'somebody' and the tendency to undertake on all occasions what is admittedly a delicate task need to receive careful consideration. Is it fair to offload on another a responsibility which one will not undertake oneself? Is it wise to rush in unless one has, after prayer and careful consideration, been led by the Holy Spirit to give the word of warning?

'Faithful are the wounds of a friend,' says the Good Book. (Proverbs 27:6.) I well remember a colleague rebuking me about an expression I had used to other members of staff: 'I don't like to hear you speak in that way concerning those men.' Though abashed, I recognised at once that he was right and felt glad that I had a friend who was not afraid to point out an error on my part. I knew he would be just as ready to defend me should the occasion demand. And I have ever been grateful to him.

Yes, 'somebody' may prove to be a true friend. There are times when we must risk accepting such an unwelcome responsibility, and not pass it on to another.

'Some people have all the luck!'

You probably don't believe in luck. A horseshoe does not hold pride of place over your front door But you will be an exception if you have not thought on occasion that someone of your acquaintance 'has it made', or a ways 'gets away with it'.

The common complaint of the delinquent schoolboy caught in the act is, 'Others do it. Why do I have to get caught?' The old Spartan outlook was that being found out was worse than the offence and gave proof of a reprehensible lack of care.

Among the ancients there was a strong feeling that a succession of favourable happenings was to be viewed with alarm – as evidence that the gods were about to intervene in a very unpleasant way.

In our day the receipt of a windfall, an apparently undeserved promotion and an escape from retribution are looked upon as enviable happenings, while the everyday progress of an apparently uneventful life marks one out as unlucky.

Very often, however, the envy which another's luck generates might well be mingled with compassion.

'Some people have all the luck!'

Experience teaches us that the man for whom everything goes well, whose prosperity and happiness seem unalloyed, often carries a secret load of care which all of fortune's favours fail to lift.

Unbroken success breeds self-sufficiency. In such circumstances it is very easy to forget God. Without him there is no future. As Jesus said: 'What shall it profit a man to gain the whole world and lose his own soul?' (Mark 8:36.) Such a person is to be pitied, not envied. Such is the position of those whose professional or financial advancement absorbs all their time and energy to the exclusion of spiritual considerations. They have swallowed Satan's bait and also his hook.

This is not to suggest that success in itself is to be deplored. Mind you, it is a heady potion. This is true even in God's service. Many a man of talent and initial devotion has lost sight of his dependence on God and has become exalted in his own eyes, developing a measure of contempt for his fellows and an unawareness of his own vulnerability. We can easily build our own little Babylons without ever experiencing Nebuchadnezzar's recovery. So let us not envy the 'lucky' one but pray rather that when all goes well outwardly the sobering thought of eternal gain or loss may act as a safeguard against self-satisfaction. If it does, then how great a benefactor of his fellows such a person may be!

'If only I had known!'

It happened during my years as a headmaster. There was a knock at my door. In response to my 'Come in', a sullen-faced lad did so and handed me a note from his teacher, asking me to discipline the boy who was making himself a nuisance in the class. I was surprised for I had always known him to be co-operative. So we got talking. Then it came out. 'Mum left us this morning,' he said, and the tears flowed.

At my request the teacher came to see me at break-time. Hearing my explanation of the apparent rebelliousness of the boy, he exclaimed: 'If only I had known!'

This is the trouble very often. We don't know all the facts, and consequently come to hasty conclusions and sometimes hasty and unwise reactions.

So many people have hidden griefs and problems. Their apparent unfriendliness or sullenness may call for sympathy and understanding rather than reproof or condemnation. When we learn the facts we are sorry that we reacted in the way we did. We too exclaim: 'If only I had known.'

Would it not be wise to exercise caution, particularly when another does not respond in the way we have learned to anticipate? A little more patience on our part and a sensitivity to another's hidden pain, whether it be physical or mental, would often avoid conflict. Indeed, it could provide balm for hurt, a release from tension and a lifting of a load. A burden shared often becomes bearable.

That was why Jesus gave the warmhearted invitation: 'Come unto me, all ye who are weary and heavy laden, and I will give you rest.'

We, his professed disciples, need to learn of him as he invited us to do. So doing, how many times we shall avoid having to say: 'If only I had known.' Instead we shall be able to give the comforting word, which may mean all the difference between despair and hope in the experience of a fellow pilgrim.

A word of caution. Do not probe. It is sufficient to show genuine interest. It will often act as a release, whereas probing may make the problem worse.

A trustful prayer, silently offered, will bring you help from heaven. God will be glad to use you to bring relief to one of his suffering children.

'How was the sermon this morning?'

The last hymn has been sung and the benediction pronounced. Now the congregation steps outside the church. 'That was good,' says one enthusiastically. 'I don't agree with what he said,' declares another. 'He shouldn't hit out at people,' comments a third. (Obviously the word had struck home.) 'I hope Mrs So-and-So was listening'; 'I like his stories'; 'At least he finished on time'. So they come, an endless variety of reactions. Who is right? How do you rate a sermon? Is it the preacher or the listener who is on trial?

There is an interesting comment on preaching in Ezekiel 33:31, 32. The comment is the Lord's to Ezekiel: 'My people . . . sit before you to listen to your words, but they do not put them into practice. With their mouths they express devotion, but their hearts are greedy for unjust gain. Indeed, to them you are nothing more than one who sings love songs with a beautiful voice and plays an instrument well, for they hear your words but do not put them into practice.'

Evidently, praise of a preacher's eloquence does not impress the Lord. What he looks for is results. What do you do in consequence of what you hear? How *do* you rate a sermon? Do you pronounce it good because you think that it will straighten out some other members of the congregation, or because it confirms your previously-held beliefs or opinions? Is it the style of the preacher, his choice of words, or his diction that wins your approval? Any one of these can be a legitimate reason for a verdict of good. But that sermon on reverence, does it bring a new sense of awe into your heart as you come into church? And the earnest appeal for all of us to spend more time in prayerful Bible study, is it still influencing your daily programme? What about that sermon which brought peace to your heart as you realised once again that so great is your Saviour's love for you that he wants to be with you all the time, if you will let him? Is it still helping you to meet life's buffetings with equanimity?

You can doubtless multiply the questions as you recall the messages God has sent to you week by week, constantly seeking to prepare you for his soon-to-be-established kingdom. The important question is obviously not whether we enjoy a sermon but what we are led to do about it. So I ask, does it depend as much upon us as hearers as upon the preacher, whether a sermon is a success or not?

'If I were you . . .'

Probably more advice is dispensed with the introductory words 'If I were you' than with any other expression. Though we may have great difficult solving our own problems, how readily we presume to place ourselves in another's shoes, to suggest a course of action which will meet the need of the moment. Not having to face the consequences of taking our own counsel, we freely give it. How often is it a case of, 'Take my advice. *I'm* not using it.'

We meet our friend's indignant narration of an unpleasant incident with, 'If I were you I wouldn't stand for it', or, in another situation, 'If I were you, I'd tell them I had enough to do already', or 'If I were you I'd have nothing to do with it'.

Given our friend's circumstances, perhaps, ultimately, we

would decide on a similar course of action. It is impossible to put ourselves totally in any other person's place. We do not know all the facts, nor do we know all the ins and outs of another's disposition. With our limited knowledge of both these factors we could very readily give counsel that would entail disastrous results.

Would it not be wiser, instead of giving our own opinion, to suggest that thought be given to how our Lord would react in such circumstances? After all, he knows all there is to know both about us and about the one or the situation that we are discussing.

So often we make the observation: 'I can't think what to do. I shall have to pray about it,' as though prayer were the last resort. Unfortunately, so often it is, but by then we have frequently complicated a situation by rash words or deeds, as difficult to recall as the proverbial feathers in the wind.

'If I were you I'd stand up for myself', or 'I'd tell her what I think of her', or 'I'd set him straight on a thing or two', we say, but how seldom these tactics result in solving a problem.

Instead they tend to alienate, to drive a wedge between the one we are advising and those with whom he has to deal. How much safer is the discretion of silence. We can so easily work ourselves up to making ill-considered statements which we afterwards regret, because we discover that the apparent slight or injustice was not intended. If it was intended, then how important it is that we should not descend to the same level of unkindness, for in so doing we but add to the injury already received.

Our Lord has a wonderful remedy for injured feelings. He invites us to spend a little while with him in our imagination as he faced provocation beyond that which falls to *our* lot. The momentary satisfaction of 'getting even' quickly evaporates when we look at ourselves in the mirror and ask ourselves: 'Did I really say that? Did I really act that way?'

So let us be on our guard. The clash of swords is not the Christian's triumph. It is the meek and lowly spirit of our Lord and Saviour, Jesus Christ.

'She's not good enough for me!'

When young people and older ones get talking together, how often you will hear some young fellow remark concerning a girl whose name has been coupled with his: 'She's not good enough for me.' Or it may be that some mother, reacting to a suggestion that a certain person might become the life companion of her son, observes: 'She's not good enough for my boy.'

Admittedly, any young Christian looking forward to marriage and recognising his responsibility towards God and his fellow men must seriously consider the character and gifts of the one who will be his partner. Wrong choices result in frustration and an inability to render to God the service which is due to him. A pretty face, a friendly attitude, and a particular gift do not guarantee a union that will redound to the glory of God.

I could wish at times, however, that the question could be: 'Am *I* good enough for *her*?' 'Is my son's character such that a young woman will be assured of a happy and successful union, one that will contribute to the well-being of the church and society?'

There are certain questions which call for an honest answer. In answering them, the modest man must be careful not to depreciate himself, and the naturally self-satisfied must be equally careful not to preen himself on what a bargain he would be to the girl lucky enough to get him. If a satisfactory answer cannot be given, then the right time to make a change is before, not after, marriage.

What are some of the questions one should put to oneself? First, am I a consecrated Christian? Am I careful, but not stingy, with money? Do I keep myself and my clothes fresh without being fastidious? Am I inclined to take the easy way out, or can I face up to difficulties and disappointments? Do I insist on having my own way? Am I a know-all, or can I learn from others? Do I know how to go the second mile without a scowl? Will the other person's reputation be enhanced by association with me?

Don't give yourself a score on all these questions. It's very difficult to be totally objective, but do give them earnest consideration. You may decide that there is marked room for improvement in some respects. Remember that the Christian can always look for and receive help from the Lord. We are not cast into a rigid mould. On the contrary, if we are willing, God will work daily to perform a miracle of re-creation in our lives.

And if our eyes are upon the right one, it will certainly be worth the effort.

 ## 'I can give as good as I get'

What a strange statement it is: 'I can give as good as I get!' Come to think of it, I have never heard it used in a positive sense, namely, to indicate a readiness to return a kindness, for example. What it usually means is that one is ready to do something or to say something equally as bad as that of which one has been the object. The expression should actually read: 'I can give as bad as I get!' But that wouldn't sound good, would it?

Returning in kind is really a poor policy. It is not calculated to solve a problem, but rather to compound it. There are then two ills to remedy instead of one. Since the initial provocation is recognised as being wrong, matching it must also be wrong. The first offence may have been unintentional. The second is calculated. The retaliation lowers one to the level of the first offender whom one has already condemned in one's own mind. No wonder the apostle Paul enjoined upon his Roman readers not to be overcome by evil but to 'overcome evil with good'. There is no doubt that such a response does something very positive in one's character development. By it one becomes recognisable as a follower of that Prince among men, our Lord Jesus Christ. For it was as a man that he demonstrated his ability to rise above provocations of every kind. However acid the term in which he was addressed, he applied the alkaline balm of his own concern for others. When sparks were flying he snuffed them out because he was not concerned to establish his own superiority, but was concerned with the salvation of others.

So next time you are tempted to give as good (or bad) as you get, substitute that which is *really* good and see if it does not prove more satisfying at the time and also have the advantage of not generating a host of later regrets. It is only too true that one can win an argument but lose a friend, which is certainly an expensive triumph and one which reveals a very poor sense of values. The use of Paul's 'coals of fire' is a remedy of proved worth and one to be highly recommended.

 ## 'I was only joking'

What is it about the expression 'I was only joking' which so often makes it suspect? The need for an explanation becomes apparent the moment the intended joke has obviously inflicted a wound causing acute discomfort to its object. When that happens we hasten to extract the barb, and that often makes matters worse, by our voicing an even more insensitive remark, such as, 'You can't take a joke', branding our victim as socially inadequate.

It often happens that what was intended only to tickle actually stings. The dividing line between those two stimuli is very narrow. The fact is that nearly always our joke is at someone else's expense, an expense that can ill be afforded.

Surely there is nothing wrong in having a bit of fun! Seeing the amusing side of things will often defuse a tense moment. A humorous comment can be very welcome. It would seem, however, that if we find it necessary to offer the explanation, 'I was only joking', there was something in our remark which had been better not said. Certainly, one is embarrassed at finding that what one has said has been taken the wrong way; that is, it has been perceived as intended to hurt.

We all have to guard against being 'thin-skinned', allowing our pride to be easily punctured. But we also have to be careful not to allow our sense of 'fun' to make us insensitive to others' feelings.

There are many factors which determine the acceptability of our 'fun'. First comes our relationship with the one to whom we are speaking. If that is intimate and warm, the danger of hurt is very slight. But if previous relationships have been distant or strained, we would do well to avoid what appears to us a harmless joke.

Our tone of voice, the set of our faces, may convey more than the actual words we speak. We must also be sensitive to the other person's circumstances and moods. Since there are often unknown factors, we need to be cautious. I well remember the reply I received one day to what I thought was a perfectly affable greeting. It was, ''Don't try to be funny. I'm not feeling like it.' It's not often that one receives such a rebuff. However, it is easy to tread on someone's corns, metaphorically speaking. So, in the interests of good relationships and the other's peace of mind, let us be doubly careful of what we say, if it may call for the explanation, 'I was only joking'.

'Don't rub it in!'

'*Now* look what you've done. You're so careless. You're always breaking things. That was my best piece of china. It's irreplaceable.' So the tirade goes on until Peter, who at first was genuinely sorry for what happened, begins to feel resentment and finally goes off in an angry mood. Added to the broken dish is the worse break of a happy relationship.

Wise is the family where it is a rule that accidents are accidents and nothing is mended by making a song about it. People are more important than things, and hurt feelings more to be regretted than the loss of possessions.

More is to be gained by sparing another's feelings than by giving expression to anger. We may think to avoid further accidents by a sharp rebuke. But the likelihood is that we shall engender a nervousness which will increase accidents rather than decrease them.

Most people feel bad enough already at having broken something belonging to another, without having their carelessness rubbed in.

It is not only material things that can get broken inadvertently. Promises and appointments can easily get overlooked, especially when emergencies arise. Failure to keep them may cause greater disappointment than the loss of some possession. Here it is well to avoid recriminations, especially those containing the word 'always'. It is so easy to use that word when the same thing has happened more than twice. We brand the offender as *always* failing in some particular, though it may not happen again for a long time, if ever. It's like having a sore finger. That's the one we seem inevitably to knock again and again. And it does hurt! But it also hurts people to be frequently reminded of a failing. Forget it, or at least don't mention it again till you have exhausted all the pleasant things on which you might comment. By then it will hardly seem worthwhile referring to it at all.

I had better stop there, or you will be thinking, 'I wish he'd stop rubbing it in!'

'Nobody can make you!'

It was an interesting sermon, well expressed and well delivered. I found myself nodding in agreement, appreciating the preacher's development of his theme. Then suddenly he rocked me with a blow right on the chin: '*Nobody* can make you lose your temper,' he declared. I swallowed hard. 'What about So-and-So?' I expostulated inwardly.

I'm afraid missed the next part of the sermon. I had to get this sorted out. 'What about righteous indignation?' I asked myself. But I knew I was evading the issue.

Losing one's temper means losing control. Who takes over in a situation like that? I like to think Jesus is in control of my life, because I have asked him to be. But I cannot expect him to do so when I let another control me. I must make my choice. Long ago he stated plainly that no man can serve two masters. I have to agree with the logic of his statement. Then where does the problem lie? As I see it, things get out of hand when we

'But!'

begin to make excuses for ourselves.

Paul had a word of warning. 'Make no provision . . . ,' he said. We need to face life with a categorical refusal to countenance in ourselves anything of which we could not expect Jesus to approve. So long as we allow ourselves the indulgence of the thought that under certain circumstances we may withdraw from our Lord's control, we open ourselves to our enemy's control. Excuses prepare the way for failure at the next encounter.

Doubtless the preacher that morning went on to develop just such an argument. He was well on with his sermon before I caught up with him. I am sure he will forgive me for that. After all, when we do not have to wait till the end of the sermon to be challenged in our thinking, we can be thankful that at some stage we have heard the authentic word of God.

We do, however, need the reassurance that Jesus will enable us to perform whatever he expects of us. It may be that his expectation of us is made clear as we read his Word, or as we pray. God gives us that reassurance in his confident statement: 'My grace is sufficient for you.'

 'But!'

How differently people use the little conjunction 'but'. It can almost be said to be an indicator of a person's outlook on life. With some it is an entering wedge to insert a generous tribute to another. Others slip it into a conversation to detract from the genuine appreciation of another which has just been expressed.

The former like to dwell on other people's good qualities. Let something derogatory be said and they will counter with, 'But you must admit they have this or that quality.' As you listen you have the comfortable feeling that your reputation is safe in their hands. They have modelled themselves on the description of the virtuous wife extolled by Solomon in Proverbs chapter 31. The twenty-sixth verse reads as follows:

> 'She speaks with wisdom,
> and faithful instruction is on her tongue.'

The habit of kindly speaking comes from a heart in which our Lord Jesus dwells. It is not an affectation. It doesn't require a great effort. It comes naturally and sweetens the atmosphere.

The contrary is also true. When others are speaking well of a person, some individuals always feel impelled to express a cautionary 'but'. Whether it is feared that their own merits will not stand comparison with those of the one mentioned, or because they have genuine fears that others are being misled, it is difficult to say, but the strange thing is that on close acquaintance one can almost predict that on some lips a 'but' will introduce something favourable, while on other lips 'but' will mean that a negative is on its way.

The negative is not always out of place. It may simply point out that it would be unreasonable to ask one already carrying a heavy load to undertake further responsibility. In that case it is indicative of a caring attitude. It would, therefore, be unwise in every circumstance to judge another by the use of the conjunction. In any case, judging is a dangerous occupation. What we need to ask ourselves is whether we have slipped into a negative rut, and, if we find we have, to pray for the love that 'thinks no evil'. (1 Corinthians 13.) It is remarkable how much brighter our days become when we practise the Christian art of kindly speech.

'I meant to'

'I meant to' is the epitaph on a host of good intentions that were stillborn. You would think that experience would teach us early in life that procrastination breeds many regrets and that – consequently – with passing years we would be wise to the necessity of doing at once what kindness or courtesy tell us ought to be done. Alas, from personal experience, I find that the missed opportunities seem rather to increase with advancing years.

The manufacturers of birthday cards have catered for this weakness in providing us with cards expressing belated greetings. Unfortunately they have no way of ensuring that belated greetings will ever reach the intended recipients.

How many accidents result from unfulfilled 'meant tos'! The hole in the ground not covered; the sharp tool left lying where little fingers can get at it; the fire left burning when a finger on the switch would have removed the danger. These and a hundred others have resulted in serious consequences to the innocent.

I've been going to write to a friend, but the weeks, the months, and even years slip by until one day the news comes through that it is for ever too late. There remain only the regrets.

Worst in human relationships are estrangements which have never been mended. I had always intended to make the first advance. Now I learn that the friend's last years were sad and dreary. Perhaps he, too, 'meant' to make it up and the old radiant friendship could have been restored. Now it's too late.

Above all the accidents, sorrows and losses already alluded to is that far greater and devastating consequence, resulting from continued delay in making the decision to listen to the voice of conscience, reminding us of the fatal outcome of failing to decide for Christ. The temptation is so strong to delay doing what we know we ought to do.

It is very easy for young people to say to themselves, 'I'm young. I want to enjoy myself. Later on, when I'm 40 or 50, then I'll turn religious.'

There are two fatal flaws in that decision. The first is that no one of us can be assured of ever reaching middle age. The second is that it is very hard to change the habits of years. The companions of today may feel cheated if we want to change suddenly from one way of life to another, and may refuse to go along with a change. Besides, if the Christian way of life does not appeal to us when we are young, on what basis can we expect it to appeal to us when we are older?

'I meant to, but didn't . . .' is fraught with many dangers. The greatest of these is the loss of eternal life through procrastination.

'It's no use talking to her. . . .'

Whether it is said in a tone of exasperation, or resignation, or despair, we know when we hear the expression, 'It's no use', that things have come to deadlock. The speaker's repeated efforts to secure a change of attitude by persuasion have been unproductive. So where does he or she go from there?

Among others there are three possible reactions. Where there is deep concern the speaker may say, 'I'll try once more. Hopefully this last attempt will have better results.' Or the expression, 'I wash my hands of the whole business', may further express the speaker's complete disillusionment. It is not a very happy expression for it implies that hands have been soiled in trying to deal with the problem. A third reaction is expressed in the words, 'I can only pray about it', as though that were the last resort, when it might well have proved to be the most effective.

Why is it that so often we turn to prayer only when

everything else has failed? Is it that we think we can manage on our own, that we should go on our own initiative? Do we think that God is the lazy man's escape from using his God-given faculties, so that we will not turn to prayer until we have exhausted every other means of achieving our objective? Wouldn't it be wiser to ask for divine help right from the beginning?

You know how it is when you use a wrong-sized spanner or screwdriver. Before you know where you are, you have burred the edges and so made your task more difficult. We do the same in our relationships when we try to solve problems with our limited knowledge and understanding. If we had asked for divine help and guidance right from the beginning, things would have gone well. By the time we get God's expertise behind us, we have already complicated matters.

So what shall we do about the one who will not listen? We'll try again, having first submitted the case to God. But we will bear in mind that since God does not employ force, we may still meet with resistance. Shall we then wash our hands of the matter? No, it is important to show our love and concern for others even when our advice is not appreciated or accepted. If we feel that a wrong course is being taken, that is all the more reason why we should keep close, so as to be on hand when help is needed. It is true that at times it is no use talking, but we can always pray.

 ## 'You made my day!'

Her exclamation resulted from such a trivial remark. She was getting on in years but her milkman had accepted payment with the words, 'Thank you, young lady.' Her face was wreathed in smiles at the implication of the term 'young lady'. 'You've made my day,' she replied and held herself a little straighter and went about her work with a lighter step.

I could not help thinking how hungry a person had to be for a little appreciation, for such a response to a happy greeting. Is it really true that people all around us are so hungry for a word of cheer? And, if it is, why are we so sparing of such expressions? Could it be that by such simple means we have it within our power to send a ray of sunshine into the dullest day of those with whom we associate. Maybe it was an exaggeration to say, 'You've made my day.' Maybe the brightness would not linger till the evening shadows fell. But her day was away to a good start.

Somehow the ordinary burdens of everyday life would not weigh so heavily and the outlook would not look so dreary, if we all adopted the habit of 'making someone's day'. It is worthwhile remembering that happiness imparted produces a chain reaction just as surely as does its counterpart. The gloom of one accentuates the gloom of another, as we all know. Just as surely, though, the sparkle in another's eyes will many a time dispel the darkness which sometimes settles on our souls at the start of the day.

But we do not have to rely on the chance remark or act of another for every day to be made for us.

Jeremiah, of all people, knew how to start every day with cheer. 'His compassions never fail. They are new every morning.' Lamentations 3:22, 23. How important it is for us to pause right at the start of the day to remind ourselves that there is One who cares. No matter what the day has in store for us, we have One who knows and understands. He has promised: 'As your days so shall your strength be.'

A concerted effort on the part of all who have tasted the love of God and the companionship of Jesus through the presence of the Holy Spirit in their lives will do much to dispel the encompassing gloom created by the horrifying news, broadcast 24 hours a day.

Maybe God will use you during this day to give just that little extra lift to your fellow worker. Maybe he will use someone else to boost you. However it is, let us all be makers of other people's days!

'Who gets the credit?'

Life seems very unfair at times. One area where this is true is in the matter of giving and receiving credit. When one knows that one person by his skill and devotion has brought a project to a successful conclusion but another is publicly thanked and commended for it, one cannot help feeling a certain indignation, all the more so when no attempt is made to put the matter straight.

This can happen in church life.

The remarkable thing about it is the fact that in the majority of cases the one overlooked is the least concerned. The reason is that his satisfaction arose not from the acclaim of others but from the knowledge that what he had set his hand to do had been achieved. That was the end of the matter as far as he was concerned.

But you may rest assured that that was not the end of it. God knows precisely what has happened and never gets mixed up over names. The final 'well done' will be addressed to the right person! And because the individual had been concerned only to do his best, the faithful servant's delight will be all the greater.

The position of the one who accepts credit for what another has achieved is a sad one. But how heartwarming it is when a man frankly disclaims credit wrongfully attributed to him and declares who should rightfully receive it. In so doing he shows himself worthy of the respect and friendship of his fellows. To accept credit which rightly belongs to another is to place oneself on a level with a receiver of stolen goods. Such a person lives in constant fear of being discovered in possession of what is not his own.

Which would you rather be? The one who is now undeservedly praised or the one who will one day hear the 'Well done, good and faithful servant!'?

Yes, it is always good to give credit to the one to whom credit is due.

'Please yourself!'

She *said* it. But that was not what she *meant*. She had wanted me to do one thing and it was evident that I was wanting to do something different. Her tone of voice made it plain that she would not be pleased if I did please myself.

On the face of it the expression 'Please yourself' is innocent enough, even generous, yet often it covers a hidden frustration or dissatisfaction on the part of the speaker, who actually wants a certain line of action to be followed while fearing that it will not be.

Is it wise to please oneself? Do we not run the risk of alienating others? When we put our own wishes foremost, giving them priority over other considerations, we often gain an empty victory. The anticipated satisfaction may easily turn to ashes in our mouths. Our circle of friends shrinks. Enjoyment which is not shared with others loses its savour. The price we pay for having our own way is costly. The anticipated elation is not realised and instead we look out on a bleak world indeed. The fact is, there is more satisfaction in pleasing others than in pleasing oneself.

To the Christian the decisive factor is whether our choices will please our Lord. He put *us* first. For the joy that was set before him, he endured the cross. From him we learn that there is fullness of joy in putting self aside that others may be blessed. In doing so we enter into a very special and intimate relationship with our Lord, which amply compensates for any momentary regret at having put our own desires to one side. Moreover, the bond which unites us with others is strengthened and friendships are enriched. We sooner or later come to the realisation that people are important, and a greater source of happiness than can come from having our own way.

The ultimate in right choices is when we really do please

ourselves when we choose to please others.

Does this mean that we should have no minds of our own, that we should always allow others' opinions or desires to determine our course of action? Certainly not. Where principles are at stake there can be only one way to go, the way that will demonstrate that our first allegiance is to God. In such circumstances there is no room for compromise.

So next time you say to someone, 'Please yourself', make sure that it's really what you mean. And when you in turn are told to 'please yourself', do make the choice which you know will meet with the approval of him whom you love, our Lord Jesus Christ.

'I've changed my mind!'

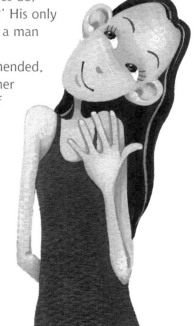

'I thought you said you wouldn't go,' he said. 'Yes, I know. But I've changed my mind,' she replied. And added with a disarming smile the way ladies do, 'That's a woman's privilege, isn't it?' His only consolation was the intimation that a man wouldn't change his mind.

That fickleness is not to be commended, all will agree. The question is whether changing one's mind is an aspect of fickleness. Let us look at the other side of the matter. Is the refusal to change one's mind an evidence of strength or of weakness? Some people's minds are like readymix concrete. Once they are set there is not much you can do about it. The imprint of an errant foot remains a permanent part of the newly-laid path. Plant an idea in some people's minds and it seems there is no way to eradicate it.

The inability to change one's mind in the light of further knowledge or changing circumstances is stultifying. It means a halt to progress. This is certainly true in the area of Christian belief and life. We need to learn to discard the good for the better.

Particularly is this true in the realm of human relationships. First impressions are difficult to remove. However, the wise man will reserve judgement and allow further acquaintance to modify or even reverse his initial judgement. Inflexibility, we often discover later, would have robbed us of friendships which later prove to be most valuable.

True, the apostle James pointed out the danger of wavering in matters of principle. Such inconsistency undermines every aspect of a man's character. No one can rely on his words for, to use a common expression, he blows both hot and cold. His responses are unpredictable. James illustrated this by citing the example of a man whose speech seems to issue from a dual source, sometimes issuing forth in sweet reasonableness and at other times in bitter utterances. Such variableness is disconcerting to say the least.

The Bible makes it plain that our minds need changing. The natural man does not think as God thinks. Until we do so we remain alienated from him. So it is that the apostle Paul bids his readers to be transformed by the renewing of their minds. (Romans 12:2.) He goes so far as to advocate our having the mind of Christ. If we do we shall certainly become godlike in our thinking. It was such thinking that enabled our Lord to see into the character of those with whom he spoke. He perceived great possibilities behind the roughest and also the most sophisticated exteriors. He saw the gold in both a Peter and a Nicodemus.

So it seems to me that once again the ladies have chosen the better part. To change their minds is not only their privilege, but it is the duty of every Christian under the power of the Holy Spirit.

'Do I have to?'

There can be few homes with young children and/or teenagers where the question, 'Do I have to?' does not come as a constant refrain. 'Do I have to put on a tie?' 'Do I have to go with you to visit Aunt So-and-So?' 'Do I have to wear a suit?' 'Do I have to clean the car?'

The questions come in an endless stream and reveal a revolt against restraints of every kind. True, in many cases the reluctance is fairly easily overcome as the reasonableness of the request is made apparent.

As the years pass, good habits tend to become established and youth conform to accepted ways without too much questioning.

However, some of us carry over this questioning attitude into adulthood and retain a rebellious attitude towards anything that or anybody who seems to be imposing a duty upon us. We want to do our own thing – or perhaps more often to do *nothing*.

Some organisations, both social and religious, impose strict rules on their members. Some even go so far as to want to impose them on all, irrespective of membership. Where belonging is a matter of choice and we know in advance what the requirements are, we really have no option other than to fall in line, at least until we have succeeded in getting the rules changed. Not to do so is to undermine the group and the result is disruptive. This is true of the Church and its constituent congregations.

With adulthood we expect conformity to established procedures which have been adopted for the well-being of the organisation as a whole. When it comes to the carrying out of plans agreed upon by those whom the members have chosen to run its affairs, conformity is essential for success. However, no plans should be made that do not allow a degree of elasticity according to the individual circumstances of its members. Compulsion does not make for peace and harmony. In matters of principle the individual should either conform or withdraw. To insist on having one's own way, contrary to the agreed procedures, creates confusion and friction.

It is not easy at times to set aside one's own preferences for the sake of unity. And none should violate his conscience in order to secure that end. It is very easy, however, to flatter oneself that one is standing fast on a principle when, in reality, stubbornness is the factor involved. We all love to have our own way. We need to examine our motives very carefully and prayerfully in order to avoid this pitfall.

Looking back over the years from the vantage point of one no longer much involved in the challenges of committee work, I have to admit that at times there was more of self than of principle in the stand I took. There must be few who, looking back over the years, have not had to come to the same conclusion.

So in our life together, and especially in our response to church life, et us not ask ourselves, 'Do I have to?' but rather, 'Is there any basis or principle for my *not* doing so?'

'No sooner done than said!'

Life is made easier when you work with people whose promises are promptly fulfilled. You can rely on their doing whatever it is they have undertaken to do. Of them it can be said: 'No sooner said than done.'

'But', you say, 'that's not the way the title reads.' Whose is the mistake? Is it the printer's or the writer's? Let's accept the inverted order of the sentence and see whether there is not a message for us in the title as it reads: 'No sooner done than said.'

'No sooner done than said!'

We live in an age which sets great store by public relations. You must advertise. Let the world know how well you do things, how superior are the goods you have to offer and how lucky people are to have you to serve them. So out with the trumpet and blow it long and loud.

How far should the Christian go along with this marketing appeal?

Very early in my Christian experience – as a child – I was made to understand the importance of reporting performance. 'How many times have you studied your Bible this week?' 'Have you rehearsed your catechism?' 'Have you prepared for confirmation class?' Thank God for concerned clergy and teachers whose aim was to establish in us good habits. The idea, as I recall, was that I should complete, each day of the week, a prescribed section in a Bible study guide.

Excellent as the habit of daily Bible study is, looking back, I realise that often my focus was on the number I could report – five out of seven, six out of seven, seven out of seven – rather than on the instruction I gained. But this was just an initiation into the reporting syndrome. There came a time when I was filling in weekly work sheets: How many visits? How many sermons preached? Talks given? Bible studies? Sick visited? Thus a friendly visit to a member became a statistic!

The accumulated statistics would make a good monthly report, and the combined reports might make us top parish in the diocese. And the purpose was unimpeachable. Clergy had to be encouraged to care for others, for, in so doing, they were fulfilling the mission of the church.

What has all this to do with our title? It has led in many

cases to an eagerness to make public any charitable action on the part of individual members or churches. Having something to report can easily become more important than the kindness itself. The deeds of some individuals or families are for ever appearing in the parish magazine. The deeds of others, done less self-consciously, go unreported and, by the doer, probably unremembered.

I wonder whether Jesus' words, 'Let your light shine before men, that they may see your good deeds and praise your Father in heaven' (Matthew 5:16) have come to mean to us, 'That they may hear or read about your good deeds.' Our Lord has said: 'Your Father, who sees what is done in secret, will reward you.' (Matthew 6:4.) Do his words not apply to us collectively as well as individually?

I'm not intending to discourage reporting. These lines are intended to remind us that if what we do is to secure the applause of men, then that is the sole reward we shall obtain. Let us be careful that others do not have cause to say of us that it is a case of 'no sooner done than said'.

'I don't care what anybody says'

If you had seen the flash in her eyes and the set of her lips as she declared her indifference to what others might say, you would not have doubted that she really meant it when she declared: 'I don't care what anybody says.'

Had she been affirming her resolute adherence to principle in the face of opposition or ridicule, one could have applauded her determination. There are times when one must take a stand or be swept away as by the strength of a powerful current. But on this particular occasion there was more of petulance than of principle as she flung the words at those around her. Indeed, the very boldness of her assertion betrayed a hidden fear that other people's opinions might

'I don't care what anybody says'

turn her aside from a course of action, the wisdom of which she herself doubted.

The plain fact is that we cannot afford under most circumstances to be indifferent to what others have to say. 'Anybody' is a very comprehensive word. It includes both friends and foes, those who love us and strangers, people of experience and those without, parents, spiritual leaders, teachers and those in authority. However much we may dislike that last word it is still there, and to flout it is to incur very serious consequences which can cause us eventually to regret having expressed ourselves as categorically as did the young lady of whom I write.

Since we do not live in a vacuum, what we do and say reacts on those around us for good or ill. We pay a heavy price for our failure to recognise this fundamental fact of life. There is no quicker route to isolation and loneliness than a disregard for other people. It takes a great deal of love to persist in trying to influence one who is determined not to hear what is said in kindness and concern. Especially (dare I say it?) when the ones concerned are older and closely related to us.

Very often their observations are born of life's experiences. They may have passed along the same road, made the same mistakes, come to the same fork in the road and gone the wrong way, only to discover how exhausting it is to have to retrace their steps with energies sapped and hopes blighted.

Naturally, if they have any esteem for others, they will want to let them profit from their own sad experience. On the other hand, they might have made a right choice and have found lasting satisfaction in the way of life chosen This they cannot impose on others, but they would be selfish indeed not to share their findings with those starting out on life's journey.

'I don't care,' can leave behind a trail of sorrowing hearts and anxious forebodings. Not to care is to brand oneself as lacking in basic human qualities. Certainly it cannot express the philosophy of one who claims to be a follower of Jesus. He cared so much that he gave up everything that most men cherish in order to bring hope into the lives of the doomed and a safe course to those adrift on the tempestuous seas of human experience.

So, don't commit yourself to being lost in a desert of your own creation constantly pursuing a mirage and never finding the true substance of life. Your family cares. Your friends care. Above all, God cares.

'It's up to you'

She was quite right, of course, when she told him he must make the decision.

He could seek advice, for mothers and fathers should lend their support to their growing and even grown-up children. But, in due course, they must stand on their own two feet.

So it was up to him.

If a foundation of right principles has been carefully laid and been backed by a consistent life on the part of the parents, they need not fear to hand over the reins at the appropriate time. And the appropriate time is when their children have demonstrated their ability to choose wisely in minor matters.

Decision-making is one of the most challenging aspects of maturing youth. There is only a very precarious future for those who cannot make up their minds. There is more than a grain of truth in the old saying, 'He who hesitates is lost.'

Every sprinter knows the importance of that first thrust against the block when the signal is given to go. Success in the race is jeopardised by even a moment's hesitation.

When confronted with temptation we dare not stop to parley. A decisive 'No' shuts the door in the face of the tempter. To hesitate is to encourage a more persuasive ploy. It's a letting down of one's guard. The enemy has already gained an advantage. Once a canoe is caught in the rapids it

'It's up to you'

takes a very skilful and experienced canoeist to avoid disaster.

But it is equally important to know when to say yes – not to temptation but to opportunity.

So many expressions have become current, handed down to succeeding generations from wise observers of the course of events in human life. For example, 'Time and tide wait for no man;' 'Seize the day!' with the implication that one is unlikely to grasp what one has first let slip by.

It might be said that it is better to make a wrong decision than to make none at all. However, this is not true when it comes to moral decisions. In the material world a temporary setback may be retrieved without too great a loss. But none can predict where the first step in an evil course may take him. Nor is it wise to defer a decision in this area.

God calls for obedience based on an intelligent weighing up of the issues involved. Observation of the evil consequences of disobedience and of the positive gains attending conformity to God's commands may bring us to the place where we shall say to ourselves: 'I will obey even though I do not fully understand the reasons for his directions.' But that is also an intelligent choice. It is one that we frequently have to make in the practical things of everyday life. How much more reasonable when we know that we are in the care of a loving, all-wise God!

But it's up to you.

'He gets on my nerves'

I caught only the last few words of a conversation between two good friends of mine. Said one: 'He gets on my nerves.' I laughed and so did they when I said: 'You've given me a title.'

It was obviously not a serious case, for they both enjoyed the rest of the evening's programme. But I fell to wondering how many people suffer from others getting on their nerves, and whether there is any way we can protect ourselves. It did not take me long to discover that very many people suffer from this complaint. Some cases are very light, but others are severe with quite drastic side-effects. After all, nerve endings are very sensitive, and when exposed they can cause considerable discomfort and pain in varying degrees of intensity.

I felt I ought to look into the matter to see if I could offer any suggestions. Diagnosis, I discovered, is easier than cure. Anyway, I thought I would have a try, for the people I hear lamenting this condition are often good friends whom I should like to help, even if I do run the risk of getting on their nerves by offering too facile suggestions. . . .

First, I'll have to admit there is not much one can do immediately about the one who gets on one's nerves. In most cases we are reluctant to tell the culprit of his or her offence. We prefer to grin and bear it, looking upon it as one of

'He gets on my nerves'

those things like gnats on a hot summer's evening which no amount of shooing or beating the air will get rid of.

So I desire to address myself to the question of the nerves. How can they be protected? Or made less sensitive? A degree of sensitivity is desirable. Its absence would bring us into the category of the thick-skinned who blunder in regardless of other people's feelings, or are quite impervious to hints that they are venturing onto dangerous ground. . . .

Nerves are frayed not by a single occurrence but by the repetition of whatever it is that offends us. Frequently we disregard our unfavourable reaction until the proverbial 'last straw'. Then, explosively, we give vent to our growing dissatisfaction and acknowledge how we feel in such terms as 'He gets on my nerves'.

Maybe it would help if we analysed our reaction at the first or second time it occurred. Did the problem lie in ourselves? Did our conscience tell us that the comment which affected us was justified? If we did nothing about it, then the repetition of the remark would naturally increase our inward discomfiture and each repetition would be more offensive.

If we decide that the first irritant was justified, we can avoid further irritation by taking action which will make its repetition inapplicable to us.

But not all situations involve us directly. Sometimes we sense that another is harming himself. We say to ourselves, with increasing vehemence, 'I wish he wouldn't.' It would take a great deal of tact and courage to draw the offender's attention to the matter, but it might be the kindest thing you could do. I write that, however, with serious misgivings, for there are those who think their mission in life is to put other people straight. . . .

There is one remedy available which is very efficacious. When we pray for someone, we enjoy peace and relaxation, for prayer is a marvellous balm for frayed nerves. If you decide to talk it over with your best friend, the Lord Jesus, the initial annoyance may well have been worthwhile.

'Oh, no! Not again!'

'What's the matter?' questions the good lady of the house at my exclamation of frustration: 'Oh no! Not again!' 'It's that firm demanding payment for a bill settled long ago. I've written to them several times, even quoting the date and number of the cheque I sent, and still these demand notes continue to arrive.'

You've probably had a similar experience. Not only firms but charities, and not only charities, but enterprising salesmen and women, who phone you in the evening under the impression that you need replacement windows every three months. . . .

And then there are the things that go wrong in the home: electric light bulbs guaranteed for a thousand hours which burn out after a few weeks. You think you have an ample supply but find they have all been used up and you are doomed to a gloomy evening till you can get to the shops again.

Life in the form of paperboys, milkmen and refuse collectors continually provokes the exclamation, a safety valve for exasperation.

Should I be very irreverent if I suggested that heaven has many occasions to use the expression: 'Oh, no! Not again'? Mind you, I'm not saying it *is* used, but it would be understandable if it were. And it is not the milkman or the postman who leaves the gate open for visiting stray dogs. It is you and I who so often do the things we have promised not to do, or fail to do what we have promised to do.

When Jesus told Peter to forgive seventy times seven, he was not speaking of an imaginary exaggerated number but, unfortunately, from experience. In his dealings with mankind over the centuries, how many times he might justifiably have reacted to our repeated failures, and in far more important circumstances than those already referred to in these lines.

This is not an attempt to justify carelessness, but simply a reminder that too strong a reaction to such minor provocations exposes us to a similar response to *our* aberrations. So the next time we have occasion to say, 'Oh, no! Not again!' let us ask ourselves, should we be addressing the words to ourselves? It may be that we shall then forget our slight provocation in the remembrance of our own guilt, and the divine forbearance from which we have profited.

Constantly we are driven to the conclusion that as God's children we should be growing into our Father's nature. It is often easy to recognise earthly parenthood, not only from the similarity of features, but also from attitudes and responses. We are encouraged to study 'to show ourselves approved unto God' (2 Timothy 2:15), and equally to study his ways and adopt them as our own.

 ## 'Take care'

Let's face it. Not many modern expressions find favour with the older generation. The complaint is that they are cheap and empty. But here is an expression to warm the heart of anyone to whom it is addressed. It lingers in the mind long after the speaker has vanished from sight.

'Take care,' say the young to the old as they leave. And there is in those two words a hint of concern for one's well-being which is like a benediction. Maybe in time it will lose its meaningfulness and be used unthinkingly. I hope not. The world of today is cold enough and indifferent enough to other people's well-being. It is refreshing to detect a note of concern in the voice of the young, a departure from self-centredness to thoughtfulness for others. It is like a caring hand placed upon one's arm.

Some reader of these lines may say to himself: 'He's just

being a sentimental old man, reading far too much into a casual remark.' Perhaps the reader is right, but it's a harmless response. You walk with some who never catch the scent of rose or wallflower, lilac or honeysuckle. Another will find delight in the scents that greet him along the way. I'm sure God made them to be enjoyed: little touches of thoughtful anticipation of his children's delight as they tread the earth in which he provided them with a home.

Warm hearts and kind words are above riches. The smile that lights up the face of a friend or that greets the stranger is like a gleam of sunshine piercing an overcast sky. It is so important to let people know that they are cared for. The modern world is far too impersonal. So many transactions are devoid of human input.

People living alone have few contacts. But they are all potential friends. That was where the charm of Jesus lay. His manner restored people's self-esteem. They knew someone cared.

It may be that *you* are living a lonely life. Your contacts with family, friends and neighbours are few and far between. You may feel that nobody cares. I've written these few lines so that you can hear a fellow pilgrim warmly say to you: 'Take care.'

'Does it matter?'

'But it *does* matter,' she retorted indignantly. My comment, intended to pour oil on troubled waters, acted more like oil added to an already flaming chip pan! It is not always the right time to express oneself philosophically about another's troubles.

Nevertheless I think we would do well to ask ourselves when vexed, 'Does it really matter?'

How often it happens in life that something which caused us to fuss (and even fume) in retrospect assumes insignificant proportions and we wonder why at the time it seemed to matter so much.

Any break from the routines of our lives can seem quite unnecessary if not positively harmful. If we have to submit, the time comes when we are equally perturbed if the new way to which we have become accustomed is changed. Reluctantly we have come to the conclusion that it was not such a bad idea after all. And now someone comes along and wants to make another change. Does it matter? Of course it does. Depending upon what it is, though, if we ask the same question in a month, or in six weeks, or in a year, we find it did not really matter at all.

Check it out for yourself. How many of the things to which you once objected have now become acceptable? Indeed, some of them have brought real benefit. The question 'Does it matter?', if used wisely, can release steam and prevent an explosion in domestic or community or church affairs. Try it.

It is not to be concluded that nothing matters. Some things do matter. A *laissez-faire* attitude *can* bring evil consequences. There are times when important principles are at stake. One of the marks of maturity is to be able to distinguish between spineless compliance and a spirited defence of the right.

I am sure that there come to your mind many situations which matter a great deal. Perhaps, like me, in many cases you feel powerless to do anything about them. Others have felt the same way, but have not been willing to accept them passively. Instead each has said to himself, 'Here is a task to be tackled, and I am going to be the one to do it.' Thus have been born many noble enterprises bringing hope and relief to thousands. But, to begin with, how small they have been. . . .

But that is the way of nature. We are born to dependency, and as strength increases we can undertake bigger things. We do not despise the baby because it cannot accomplish what a grown-up can. Neither should we despise the early efforts of those who apply themselves to the remedying of things that really matter. And there are so many of them.

So let us not waste our strength and sympathies on that which in a little while we shall recognise as not really mattering, and reserve our energies for those things that really *do* matter.

 ## 'I can't complain'

You could hardly say that he bubbled over with enthusiasm, which was surprising since the ensuing conversation revealed that in many respects things had gone very well for him.

It turned out that he and all his family had escaped the flu bug which had brought distress to many families. Business had been brisk and the bills he had had to pay for various repairs had been lower than he had anticipated. All this came out afterwards. But his initial answer to my question, 'How are things?' had been the somewhat lugubrious, 'I can't complain'.

It was not as though he was one of the heathen. Had he been in that category he might have feared that the gods,

'I can't complain'

hearing a positive statement of contentment, might have decided it was time to reverse the order of things and let troubles dominate his life for a while lest he be carried away with his good fortunes. No. He had no such fears. The expression he used was, it seems, his superlative in the way of gratitude and appreciation.

Many people seem to have a fear of admitting that they have been well treated and have cause for rejoicing. 'Not so bad,' they say when you might have expected an expression of complete satisfaction. Their admission that they have no reason for complaint is to inform you that they are seldom in the position when life has dealt so kindly with them and that, contrary to the usual run of things, they have had a very fair deal.

They would modify their statement at times by the addition of the words 'on the whole' so that you would understand that things were not perfect, but since they were not too difficult to please, they would dismiss minor reasons for complaint by the expanded statement, 'I can't complain *on the whole*'.

I'm not sure that it is fair for me to write this in the third person. I mean, it could well be that at times my own speech is lacking in expressions of enthusiastic appreciation. . . .

So, in face of this fact, I should perhaps change to the first person, in rebuking this rather grudging response to God's goodness, and say *we* ought to be more positive. The declaration of that goodness does our own souls good, as well as directing a ray of joy into the lives of others. Indeed, a lilting melody does more to lighten weary feet and limbs than does a dirge. And, to be honest, the Christian must recognise that he enjoys much that is foreign to those who do not know that they are the children of a very loving Heavenly Father. One can face the difficulties that arise in the prosecution of any enterprise with equanimity when one is assured of its successful outcome.

The greatest undertaking in life is to attain a righteous character which will fit one to live in a perfect environment with perfect people for ever. But you say: 'That is just the trouble. I find such a character very elusive.' Then you'll need to do what I've had to do: admit your inability to attain it on your own, and accept as yours the perfect righteousness of the Lord Jesus Christ. This is God's free offer. Surely we can't complain about that!

'Goodbye'

Like many other expressions, 'Goodbye' has suffered greatly from its careless use. Have you ever stopped to think that this term is a contraction of the phrase 'God be with you'? People use it despite the fact that they give little or no thought to God, and those to whom it is addressed are not impressed that they have been entrusted to God's care. It is interesting that the later languages also invoke God's protection on parting guests. 'Adios' say the Spaniards. 'Adieu' say the French.

How heart-warming it would be if these words which speed our friends on their way were spoken and accepted with a full realisation of their meaning. The hazards of life are very real and imminent. Does the wish 'God be with you' mean that we are exempt from all ills? Certainly the thoughtless use of the term by those who do not reverence God or trust to his love cannot mean anything positive in the lives of those so addressed. But supposing, after having said goodbye, the next thing we learn is that death has stepped in to end the present relationship, does that mean that our farewell was ineffective? I think not, for I recall the confident words of the psalmist David: 'Even though I walk through the valley of the shadow of death, I will fear no evil, for you are with me; your rod and your staff they comfort me.' (Psalm 23:4.)

What a marvellous concept that is. God with us in 'death'.

Or, to be more precise, when we pass through the valley of the shadow of death. The explanation is that, as Jesus said, the end of this present life is not death in the ultimate sense. It is only a sleep from which we shall awake when Jesus comes. If we have had Jesus with us before we 'go to sleep', Christ's resurrection is the guarantee that we shall rise again to a real existence. After that, goodbyes will have nothing tentative about them. We shall for ever dwell in the presence of the holy one.

An old song ran: 'Say au revoir, but never goodbye'. But the Christian can be assured of that 'revoir' as he says his goodbyes, providing both he and the one from whom he is parting have committed their ways to God, whose eternal purpose is that we shall enjoy eternal life with him.

So, to you all, I say, 'Goodbye.' God be with you.

'I've made up my mind'

Decision-making is a vital factor in life. Every child needs to be taught how to go about this important element in the totality of life's responses, with which we are all confronted. Inability to make up one's mind makes for vacillation, and vacillation leads to lost opportunities and exposure to grave dangers. So when we hear a firm, 'I've made up my mind,' it is often a ground for rejoicing.

Unfortunately it is very easy to make up one's mind without weighing up all the factors involved and carefully calculating the consequences. Snap decisions lead to vain regrets, so it is important to study carefully the factors that have led to the decisions we make, to see whether they warrant the conclusion.

In my mind's eye I see the owner of a business sitting at his desk and carefully reviewing the factors affecting his trade. Can the adverse trends be remedied? What measures can he take to balance his accounts more successfully? Are some things out of his control? How many people's lives suffer from his decisions, or can he enhance their happiness and prosperity by taking the appropriate measures?

Looking back over my own life, I have to recognise that while I made up my mind in certain circumstances I did so on impulse rather than principle. I failed to consult the One who has a vital interest in my life and in the lives of those who would be affected by my decision. Looking back I can see that it would have been wiser and kinder of me, in some cases, to have delayed carrying out my decision until I had had time to consider carefully the consequences, and had given my Mentor time to enlighten me on its effects.

Having said this, I must nevertheless applaud the action of the person who makes up his mind without reservation where principles are involved. None of us can afford to shilly-shally on such matters. Our arch-enemy knows that if we once begin to hesitate it is likely to weaken our resolve, causing us to compromise. But there is no halfway house in the choice between good and evil.

Indecision results in so many losing their mastery of life's circumstances. They become entangled in the devil's snares, believing that they have chosen the way of enjoyment only to discover, too late, that they have become the victims of a delusion.

I love the robust declaration of Joshua as recorded at the end of the book bearing his name. He declared: 'As for me and my household, we will serve the Lord.' (Joshua 24:15.) He made up his mind on the side of right, and his decision was not to be changed by the behaviour of others.

'You never know'

Life presents us with many surprises. Sometimes help comes from a source where we least expect to find it. Sometimes the reverse is true. That is why, as Christians, we commit ourselves into God's hands every morning. He knows what the day will bring of trial and opportunity. He is not caught off guard. If we keep in close contact, he will be able to prompt us with the right reaction to every situation that arises. He can turn the most unpromising of circumstances to his glory. Remember God's glory is his power to deliver Satan's captives from the prison of sin and he can use us, his children on Earth, in the accomplishment of that purpose.

The Wise Man urged his readers to be diligent in sowing at all times, since the results were unpredictable to man but not to God. (Ecclesiastes 11:1-6.) In the exercise of hospitality, the letter to the Hebrews reminds us that we may entertain angels unawares. (13:2.) Better still, our Lord tells us that we may ultimately find that the stranger we entertained was our Lord himself. (Matthew 25:37-40.)

What we term 'coincidence' is very often God's planning. The 'chance' encounter may be God's answer to our morning prayer. Incidents which we have long since forgotten may have exerted an influence for good or for evil which comes to light only many years later. You never know.

Your word of sympathy, your act of simple honesty when you might have got away with it, may weigh in the balance of another's life to turn the scales in favour of truth and righteousness.

One of the happiest surprises awaiting the redeemed when they reach God's eternal kingdom is to have someone come and say: 'Do you remember encouraging me one day when I was on the point of giving up? I did not immediately respond to your words or your kindness, but God used you that day to help overcome Satan's attempts to drag me down into the pit of hopelessness. Thank you.'

In my sixty-odd years as a Christian – and as a pastor – I have found that it is not the closely-reasoned sermon that has necessarily meant the most to me. Rather, it has been some insight or simple statement that caught my imagination and challenged me to a more responsive attitude towards Christian living. One such occasion was when I read a recent editorial in a Christian paper where Jesus was represented as talking with Gabriel as they viewed the empty mansions he had gone to prepare. Jesus asked: 'Gabriel, don't they *want* to come home?' The pathos of that question went to my heart and evoked the response: 'Yes, Lord, I do want to come home.'

Our Christian pilgrimage together is a 'battle and a march'. You never know just how heavy the pack on another's back may be. He may be almost falling beneath the load. Perhaps your word, your outstretched hand, your expression of care, may be just what is needed to brace the tired muscles, to quicken the resolve, so that he will reach the end of the road and have a part in the grand victory parade in God's kingdom. You may not know now, but you will know then.

'I don't feel like it!'

How many challenging situations we avoid with the words 'I don't feel like it!'

Those words are the enemies of achievement, the passport to physical and mental inertia. Once they take control in our lives, creativity is inhibited. We begin to vegetate.

It is particularly easy to fall back on this formula at times of physical weakness. Any effort daunts us. We would rather let things drift than put forth the effort to deal with them.

'I don't feel like it!'

Sadly, the more often we fall back on this expression, the more readily it characterises our reaction to all kinds of situations. There is really only one way to combat this deadly lethargy and that is by resolutely tackling some task which initially gives rise to this response. If we will do so the paralysis will be broken and we shall feel the first stirrings of enabling energy.

As artificial respiration leads to a resumption of normal breathing, so the resolute tackling of some minor task and its accomplishment will set in motion the impulses which formerly functioned so well and we become, once more, not the slaves of our feelings, but masters in our own lives.

How inspiring it is to hear and read of those who have overcome handicaps to accomplish tasks which their more fortunate fellows have failed to achieve simply because they never braced themselves. As a young man I had a companion, for a while, who made a practice of responding promptly to every call of duty. It was no surprise to me to see him entrusted with ever wider responsibilities. Where others spent their energies in a search for excuses for not doing what was required of them, he did not give excuses time to develop but immediately got to work. Consequently in a very short time the task was behind him and did not take a toll of his resources.

After weeks of illness or, perhaps, that 'old-age feeling', we feel that our energy has been sapped. 'I don't feel like it!' becomes almost a routine reaction. Every task is a burden. I have found this myself.

As one who frequently dispensed good advice to others, I resolved that I had better begin at home. These lines contain no remarkable revelation of truth. But writing them has, itself, been therapeutic. It has also made me realise the wisdom of the old saying, 'Well begun is half done.'

'Mind where you're going!'

The irate injunction swallowed up my confused apology for having inadvertently bumped into the good lady laden with parcels.

'Mind where you're going,' she said.

And she was right.

I needed to come out of my forgetfulness of my surroundings and pay attention to my movements, not only for the sake of other people but also for my own sake.

In a broader sense there is, in this, a message for every one of us. As we tread life's path it is very easy to lose sight of where that path is leading us. It takes only a slight initial deviation from strict honesty in business dealings to set us on the way to major concessions to what we come to consider necessary acts of misrepresentation. Eventually we can find ourselves so entangled in duplicity that we can see no way out. It is, therefore, of paramount importance that we mind where we are going or, as the Scriptures say, the price may be the losing of our souls.

The student is faced with a similar danger. He may start off in his studies with great diligence, faithfully performing the tasks allotted to him. Then comes the day of the first neglect. It does not seem to incur any penalty. Gradually he may become less and less conscientious in his preparation until finally the gulf between knowledge and bluff becomes too wide to bridge and he becomes a drop-out.

In the realm of the Spirit, the hazards are equally great. Pressures of work, of appointments, bring about an occasional neglect of prayer and Bible study. Unless we mind where we are going, we soon find the ratio of missing either of these essentials to spiritual health gradually increases until, instead of the neglect being only occasional, the performance becomes more and more rare. The resultant spiritual anaemia will bring us to the place where we have no appetite for spiritual things. From *missing* church only rarely, we find ourselves *attending* only rarely, until we become only names on the church register and strangers in the church itself.

If, on reviewing the situation, we discover we are off course, let none of us accept Satan's usual assertion that it is too late; things have gone too far; there is nothing we can do about it. These statements are in keeping with his character as the father of lies. Jesus declared, 'I have come to save the lost.' A man is not lost until he sees no way of getting back onto the right path. If that is your position, you are just the one whom Jesus came to rescue. Don't think that he will be nagging you all the way back. He calls us the sheep of his pasture. There's no point in nagging a sheep! Let him pick you up and bear you back to safety. He will do it joyfully.

You will mind where you are going, won't you?

'Welcome!'

There are few words to which our hearts respond more readily than the word 'Welcome'. It belongs to a smiling face and an outstretched hand; to eyes that light up with pleasure at our approach. It banishes all hesitancies and misgivings. It transforms a stranger into a friend.

There are many words in our dictionaries and indeed in common speech with which we would gladly dispense. But not this one. In its absence the sunlight would fade from our encounters and a chill as of a passing thunder-cloud would fall upon us.

However long the journey, however arduous, as this word falls from gracious lips, only the joy of the present remains. Banished are all thoughts of the wearisomeness of the way.

When one travels abroad where the language of the

people is unknown to the traveller, there is one time when an interpreter is not needed. A friendly welcome is its own interpreter of the spoken word.

In church life, how important it is that the visitor be greeted with a genuine word of welcome and a handshake that communicates the pleasure that his or her presence affords to the regular member. The sense of belonging which such a welcome conveys puts one in the right frame of mind to receive a spiritual blessing from the ensuing service. And the warm 'come again', which falls on the visitor's ear on departure, lingers as an added benediction, enfolding him or her in the circle of God's family.

If this is true in our relationships on Earth, and true it is, what about the word of welcome which will fall upon our ears at the end of life's journey, when we stand at the portal of the eternal city and our glorious Host declares his joy that we have come? He will have waited a long time for that glad moment. No hard scrutiny awaits us. No cold questioning look to challenge our right to be there. We shall be greeted by name, our special name which grew out of our relationship with our Lord through the years.

'Come in,' he will say. 'I've been preparing for your arrival. Let me show you around.'

Stop and picture the occasion. Let the thrill of it carry you away. You'll forget the difficulties of the journey in joyous anticipation of that welcome. It will not be just a welcome *en bloc*. It will be personal and heartfelt.

In our present life most of us have, at times, received rebuff where we had anticipated a welcome, been received as an enemy when we have called at a house in a spirit of friendship. But there is no danger of that. We shall not even be welcomed as guests, because we shall be welcomed as children coming home from a long absence. Jesus will be there to tell our heavenly Father that we've arrived. There will be no sulking elder brother there, envious that we are receiving so warm a welcome. So generous is the spirit of heavenly beings that they will spontaneously burst into songs of joy and welcome.

Let us show now in the way we welcome others that we have already entered into the spirit of heaven, which values others as Christ has valued us in giving himself for our redemption.

'I'm sorry'

'I'm sorry you were put to so much trouble.' 'I'm sorry I could not help you.' 'I'm sorry you could not come.'

I'm sorry for this and sorry for that.

The expressions are endless and the sorrow is usually very superficial. It may denote a degree of resistance or even defiance. For instance when a 'but' follows. 'I'm sorry but you really cannot expect me to comply with your request or expectation.' How glibly the words slip out and how little they mean.

It is altogether different when they are spoken on their own. How meaningful they become and how healing they are, but how much harder to say. There is in them a wealth of meaning. Their sincerity awakens a reassuring response far beyond that resulting from a multiplicity of words of explanation. There is in them the sincerity of regret, a confession without any element of self-justification. Perhaps that is why we are slow to use them. Try saying them on their own. Note the overtone of caring that creeps into them.

Don't overdo it, however. Don't think that saying 'I'm sorry' excuses you from keeping a close check on your words and actions. Frequent repetition will rob your words of that ring of genuine regret which brings conviction and readiness to forgive. Make sure that you are not using them simply as a line of defence against the unpleasant consequences to yourself of the initial offence, and don't get on your high horse if the response is not as gracious and spontaneous as you would like it to be. If you then retort, 'I've said I'm sorry, haven't ?' you may make matters worse. You haven't really paid your debt by saying 'I'm sorry', but you have opened the way for the offended one to experience the balm of forgiveness. For when we forgive we do ourselves more good than we do the offender. We enter into the mind of our Lord. He never wanted to wear the horsehair shirt of antagonism to his enemies and still less of estrangement from his friends.

I hesitate to mention one aspect of this subject lest it be seized upon as a pretext for insensitivity. But mention it I will. There are times when we know that what we have to say may give offence. We are indeed sorry for that, but because we care we feel it is our duty to warn another of the evil consequences of his or her course of action. This calls for great tact, a complete lack of self-righteousness, and a heart of love. Let us beware, however, of earning the reputation of being a setter of other people right. . . .

'So-and-so ought to read that . . .'

It is remarkable how appropriate some things we hear or read are for *other* people, or so it seems to us.

They hit the nail right on the head, exposing *other* people's foibles so aptly.

It is good to have a mind for others, but we can do so to our own loss. A very revered pastor used to advise his hearers: 'Use a rake and not a pitchfork.' In other words, take the message to yourself and do not immediately think of someone else who will benefit from hearing the admonition. There is no surer way of losing a needed blessing than to sidestep it and, with skilful action, make a clever pass to someone else.

Admittedly we do it with the best of intentions, but the

'So-and-so ought to read that...'

probability is that we have been subconsciously focusing upon what we feel is a blind spot or misconception in another person's experience. We may not have expressed it openly, but we have felt how much better he would be if he could become aware of a particular failing or illogical attitude. What we have just read or heard appeals to us as being the precise antidote.

It has often been said that the weaknesses in others are, in many cases, precisely those in our own lives. That being the case, we should do well to respond to the revelation that comes to us and allow it to alert us to our *own* need.

He who listens to a sermon or reads an article sensing only how it fits another's need, without first applying it to his own, can eventually become the victim of this habit and so deprive himself of the very help of which he stands in need. This is no new thing. It has unfortunately characterised generation after generation of men and women. Only a resolute determination to seek the plank in our own eye, to use our Lord's expression, will save us from 'quenching the shafts of truth which God directs on us to the saving of our souls'.

What should we consider the best kind of article or sermon? Is it the one which confirms us in our present understanding or attitude, or is it the one which makes us squirm? A correct diagnosis of a potentially dangerous condition is not to be despised.

This in no way detracts from the value of material which builds up our faith in the truths of God's Word. Indeed we need them both, the probing and the confirming.
So it is that there are times when we can sincerely say: 'So-and-so ought to read this,' for we have already experienced its beneficial effect in our own lives.

'Don't pray this prayer, unless . . .'

What comfort we Christians take from the statement made by the aged apostle John in his first epistle (chapter 1:9), that if we confess our sins he (God) is faithful and just to forgive us our sins and to cleanse us from all unrighteousness. We realise that without forgiveness we cannot hope to have a place in the heavenly kingdom.

What puzzles me is that so many people frequently pray not to be forgiven. I'm not speaking of the heathen or the unbeliever, but church members who are regular in attendance and who join in congregational responses. Probably the most frequently-used prayer is the one that our Lord Jesus gave as a model to his disciples at their request. Yet I contend that there are times when we are very unwise to pray that prayer!

Indeed, it is positively dangerous to do so!

I am not for a moment suggesting that there is anything wrong with the prayer. But let me remind you of part of its wording. I quote from the King James Version (Matthew 6:12): 'And forgive us our debts, as we forgive our debtors.' It's the second clause of this petition which worries me: 'As we forgive our debtors.'

Not long ago I heard a member declare concerning a sister in the church: 'I'll never forgive her.' Yet at the close of the pastoral prayer in the service which followed, that member joined with the others in repeating the Lord's Prayer, including the clause to which I have referred. Then that prayer became a deliberate request not to be forgiven, with all the consequences of such a request. That's why the title of this piece: 'Don't pray this prayer, unless . . .'. Unless what? Unless the petitioner has forgiven the one who has sinned against him or her. How dreadful it would be if God took us at our word when we pray that prayer without first forgiving, for it would mean our exclusion from heaven.

This was a subject to which our Lord returned on a number of occasions. Most notably, perhaps, in the story he told of a servant who, having been forgiven a colossal sum, showed himself merciless towards a fellow servant whose debt to him was trivial in comparison (Matthew 18:21-35). His master retracted his forgiveness and the servant had to suffer the consequences.

We may be inclined to think of this as an isolated incident, but actually Jesus was including all of us in his condemnation if, having received God's generous forgiveness of our multiple sins, we cannot find it in our hearts to respond as graciously to those who offend us. Even our offerings are unacceptable to him until we have done our best to establish right relations with others.

Indeed, the praying of the Lord's Prayer should bring to us a wonderful feeling of relief, the lifting of the load of guilt from our shoulders, and provide an 'open sesame' to the hearts of our fellow believers.

In conclusion, let me change my exhortation to, 'Do pray this prayer', knowing in your hearts that you also have freely forgiven as God, in his mercy, has freely forgiven you.

 # 'I'm bored!'

Of all the people who have a claim on our sympathy, those with the greatest claim are the ones who are constantly bored. Victims of illness or accident frequently rise above their problems, but there seems no escape for the ones who suffer from boredom.

There are those who are 'bored to death' by a stay in the country. Lacking the stimulus of city traffic, lights and entertainments, for them life becomes a drab monotony. Where others find delight in woodland and meadow, on hillsides and in dales, the sufferers from boredom shrink from finding the same scene before their eyes day after day.

Others find church services boring. The familiar pattern evokes in them a feeling of revolt. They can eat the same kinds of meals day after day but the same kind of service once a week brings on a severe bout of self pity. It really is very sad.

Strangely enough, those suffering from this malady often mistakenly attribute their state of mind to intellectual superiority, instead of recognising it for what it really is, a probable evidence of spiritual apathy. They obviously have no inner resources on which to draw. Consequently, in the absence of a constant variety of changing stimuli, they have nothing on which mind or spirit can seize to occupy their attention. They enter the house of God where he has promised to be present but, lacking the eye of faith, they fail to discern him before whom heavenly hosts fall prostrate. Oh, for the vision that allows us to see the Unseen and hear his voice in the reading of the Scriptures.

Fortunately it is not necessarily a terminal condition. Expanding horizons and wider experience will, in time, create an inner world to which the sufferer can retreat. Indeed it is possible to create an antidote to this condition. Here are three suggestions. The first is to create a mental picture of God in his majesty on which we can focus when immediate circumstances fail to capture our attention. If we will allow our minds to dwell on Isaiah's vision recorded in the first few verses of chapter 6, and reinforce the picture by dwelling on John's visions as related in Revelation 4, we will have constantly before our eyes such a scene as will dispel any threatening boredom.

The second suggestion is to fill one's memory with such striking passages as 1 Corinthians 13, comparing the standard set there with its fulfilment as recorded in Isaiah 53.

A third area of retreat from boredom is to acquaint oneself with outstanding passages from the great oratorios so that the inner consciousness reproduces both the vocal and the instrumental resonances which lived in the minds of the great composers.

Each of these suggestions makes demands on one's powers of imagination and concentration, but the result is that one can live in a realm of glory which makes one oblivious of mundane and boring circumstances.

Like cures for all kinds of maladies, the prescription must be adhered to constantly until eye and heart and mind are irradiated by the glory which is ever with one.

This is an unfailing remedy for boredom. If you don't choose to use it, beware of betraying yourself by saying: 'I was bored.'

 ## On taking offence

Some call it wearing one's heart on one's sleeve. Others describe it as being touchy. However you may choose to describe it, it certainly accounts for many alienated friendships.

People decide that it is safer to keep at a distance from those who easily take offence. They do not necessarily respond in kind, but are careful not to become involved with those who are volatile.

I don't suppose many of us sit down to give the matter serious consideration, neither those of us who tend to respond quickly to an apparent slight, nor those of us who feel that there is nothing to be gained by pursuing a relationship where sparks fly for what appears to us to be no reason at all.

A friend of mind pointed out that the offender probably had no idea that he had spoken or acted unwisely, and certainly had no intention of hurting. In that case surely the best thing to do is to assume the best and continue the relationship as though nothing had happened. Why lose a friendship without a cause? On the other hand, he said, if offence were intended, the golden rule established by our Lord himself is to forgive – not merely for the sake of the offender but for one's own sake.

There is nothing that casts a deeper shadow over a day than to go through it with a nagging resentment eating away one's vitality. You say, 'I can do that once or twice, but when it happens repeatedly I draw the line there.' That's when we have to begin looking within. We then become aware that we have had to ask for forgiveness more times than we care to remember. Nevertheless, we have accepted God's assurance of forgiveness, realising that we have needed it not once or twice but on numerous occasions. And he has told us that we can have it only on the basis of acting towards others as we want him to act towards us.

My friend added that if the intention had been really to hurt then we should feel for the perpetrator, since he was doing himself more harm than he was inflicting on others.

It is possible to harm other people's reputations but, thank God, no one can spoil our characters. They are in our keeping. That is why I say that those who intentionally say hurtful things are their own worst enemies. Reputations can be regained but it is a much harder thing to mend characters. In the end we shall not be judged by what we are reputed to be, but by what we really are.

So do not let us allow the slights and hurts inflicted on us to trouble us too much, but let us have a thought for their originators.

'Who would have thought it?'

The news spread rapidly. They stood in amazed and bewildered knots discussing what they had just learned. Such terms as 'Incredible', 'I can't believe it', 'Who would have thought it?' dominated the conversation. Then gradually another note began to creep in. The more sophisticated began to recall little incidents, passing remarks, which lent credence to the report. 'I always thought there was something not quite right,' says one. 'Do you remember such-and-such an occasion?' adds another.

Gradually the matter is rationalised, until incredulity gives place to confirmation and confirmation to condemnation. Hearts that had first rejected the implications of the news close to sympathy and open to cynicism.

The majority have already decided that the gossip must be true, and the verdict has to give way to determining what retribution should be meted out. Anyone interjecting a word of caution will be suspect: 'Where are your standards? Can't you distinguish between right and wrong?' Coldness splits up the group. 'I can't understand how you can take such a position.' Brotherly love dies on the scaffold of suspicion.

It's an old story. We've all heard it many times. And – dare I say it? – had a share at times in the decision-making and execution. Then, perhaps, on returning home, we have looked into the mirror and thanked God that *our* secret has not become public property. . . .

That's why Jesus has my admiration. When they brought him a woman notorious for her loose living, he was not interested in hearing the details. Nor did he tell the onlookers the sins of her accusers. 'Neither do I condemn you,' he declared. (See John 8:1-11.)

It was the same at the Last Supper. Though aware of the treachery of Judas, Jesus did not expose him. Love still triumphed in his heart. Sadly it was not met with an answering love.

'Love covers a multitude of sins,' says the Good Book. It can also facilitate a cure. It does not necessarily produce instantaneous results. Indeed, we may never know in this life how the poisoned well of another's life was sweetened by a generous word or action.

Have you ever stopped to think what havoc God could cause in our congregations? He knows every detail of our lives. Supposing he were the kind of God who took delight in our confusion and shame? But he isn't. And we as his sons and daughters should learn from his example and not feed on others' mistakes.

There's another side to all this. Who would have thought that the boy or girl who caused the church members and parents so much anxiety, who refused to conform to accepted standards of dress and deportment – would one day prove to be such a powerful influence for good? What brought the change? Not denunciation and despair, but the love of Jesus which, received into the heart, can transform the life.

Who would have thought that he would have set his love upon us and expended so much effort to make sure we spend eternity with him?

'Can you tell me the way?'

How often when you accost a passerby on the street saying, 'Excuse me, but can you tell me the way to, . . .' before you have finished the question the person will reply: 'I'm sorry, but I'm a stranger here myself.'

Occasionally, in towns frequented by tourists, the one questioned will add, 'But wait a minute, I've got a street map here. Perhaps we can find the place

'Can you tell me the way?'

you want and the way to it.'

Sometimes the reply will be a complex succession of lefts and rights, until, noticing your growing bewilderment, your informer will change tactics and say, 'I'm going that way myself. Just come with me and I'll put you right on the spot.' What a relief! A guide is so much better than someone giving directions. The latter can so easily forget, as he gives you directions, that at a certain junction there are two roads to the right or left. His familiarity with the route makes him oblivious to the problem another will face when he reaches that point.

Meditating on this not infrequent happening, I asked myself how ready am I to direct travellers along life's highway? Do I have to confess that I am a stranger needing to be directed by another, instead of being in a position to give clear directions? Have I learned to consult my Guidebook written by One who found his way and has promised to be a Guide to all intent on reaching the gates of the golden city? Do I try telling others the way they should go and perhaps make it sound so complicated that they throw up their hands in despair? Or can I say, 'That is my destination too. Let's go together. And, as we go, let's consult the Good Book.'?

Bunyan's Pilgrim was often sidetracked. At times his attention was caught away by the things happening around him, momentarily so fascinating, so desirable. Much time was lost as a result. His strength was sapped; he grew faint and discouraged. The road seemed to drag on endlessly. Just when hope seemed to have vanished, help would come and he would press on his way again.

We have One who sticks closer than a brother. If we will allow him to teach us, we shall pursue our journey more resolutely. Hand in hand with other seekers we shall tread the appointed path, encouraging one another as we pass the landmarks so clearly indicated in our Guidebook. Each, in turn, will cheer the seekers. The night of our journey is far spent. The dawn of eternal day brightens the distant horizon.

We remember the rapturous welcome awaiting us. The lurking foe is not forgotten, but he that is for us is stronger than he that is against us. Our safe arrival is assured.

When the stranger stops you to ask, 'Excuse me, can you tell me the way?' will you lamely say, 'I don't know'? or will you say, 'I'm going there myself. I have a Guidebook and a Guide. Let's go together'?

'There's so little I can do'

Day by day we are confronted by the limitless needs of the many for comfort and material help. Eventually we have a sense of helplessness in the face of their problems. To add to those we encounter in everyday life, news of overwhelming disasters involving millions of people comes to us every day. We look at our meagre resources of health and wealth, of talent and skill, and despair of making any worthwhile contribution. Old age, poverty, disabilities of one kind or another, and the inescapable responsibilities which seem to exact every ounce of our energies, evoke the sorrowful cry: 'There's so little I can do.'

Yet we learn how much the severely handicapped achieve on behalf of their fellows. We wonder at the strength of their motivation, and discover that far from exhausting themselves many generate new strength and abilities.

The natural world is full of examples of how, by corporate activity, the smallest creatures can achieve amazing results. Think for example of the coral reefs of the Pacific Ocean. These are the product of millions of creatures whose individual contribution is minute.

In this country we daily read of the accomplishments of the most severely handicapped. I think at this moment of David who has grown up a victim of muscular dystrophy which has confined him to a wheelchair with only the minimal use of his hands. He has every reason to say, in view of his circumstances: 'There's so little I can do.' In middle age he was received into a Cheshire Home, apparently totally dependent on others, but he has brought into it such a spirit of cheer and optimism that instead of being considered an additional burden he has brought life and cheer, not only to his fellow patients but also to the staff.

How, then, can we who have the use of our faculties sit back and say: 'There's so little I can do'? We have but to look around us to find opportunities for service, and in that service self-fulfilment.

Our contribution to life may be small, but the totality of our achievements will be such as to form another wonder of the world. Start doing little things. Indeed you may never get beyond little things, but in the aggregate they will result in benefit to others beyond your expectation *and* be an inspiration to many. Jesus voiced his approval of the contributions made by an impoverished widow because she did the best she could, and heaven records no greater accolade than the one she received from the Lord of the universe. She had done what she could.

You may be quite right when you say: 'There's so little I can do.' But however little it may be, do it!

 ## 'He's very ambitious, you know'

We sat chatting, a group of senior citizens. The name of a certain young man cropped up and the statement was made: 'He's very ambitious, you know.'

I could not detect whether the speaker's remark was made in commendation or disapproval. I fell to pondering the question of ambition, whether it is desirable or otherwise. I thought back over those I had known over the years who could have been described as ambitious. They automatically fell into one or other of two categories.

There were those who were ambitious for self, and those who were ambitious for service.

I found myself applauding the drive and application which characterised the ambitious. They set themselves a goal and pursued it single-mindedly. So far so good.

Then I went on to think of where their ambitions had led them and the types of people they had become. I decided that ambition could make a man fit for the world to admire, but unfit for heaven. But it could also fit a man for success in this life and create a character that God would gladly welcome into the world to come. The divergence is quickly discernible.

Undoubtedly we are held responsible for the development of the talents entrusted to us. Long years of teaching have revealed to me that those who conscientiously apply themselves with a view to serving God and their fellows do not have to wait till a future life in order to have further responsibilities entrusted to them. Even in this life abilities are conferred upon them which were not in evidence in the early stages of their experience. Moreover, those with whom they are associated are enriched, not only by their skills but by the warmth of their personality.

How different it is with those whose ambition is only for personal gain or glory. Achieve they may in the particular field of their endeavours, but their very achievements erect a barrier between them and their fellows.

In the parable of the talents Jesus stated that those who had used them wisely brought their gains to their master, recognising that what they had

gained resulted from what they had first been given. So too will all true-hearted followers of Jesus gladly return to their Lord the gains he has enabled them to make. Their success does not lead them to boastfulness or a sense of personal superiority.

Too often those whose ambition has been for personal gain or glory look with disdain upon their fellows from whom they become separated. This separation leads to separation from God. They lay up treasure for themselves on Earth – wealth and applause – but their deposits in the bank of heaven are meagre indeed.

These were my thoughts as I sought to analyse the intent of the remark made casually concerning one young man. What of you? Are you ambitious? I hope so, but with a godly ambition.

 ## 'It'll do'

When I tell you that I grew up in the era of brass fenders, shovels, kettles and tongs, you will perhaps think of me also as being a museum piece.

Now those brasses needed to be polished fairly frequently and my mother considered the task well within the range of her youngest's abilities. When I had finished she would cast her eye over the fire-irons and usually see room for improvement. She was not impressed by my claim, 'It'll do, won't it?' and taught me that anything but the best is not good enough.

Through the years I have come to realise that 'It'll do' is the road to mediocrity, and gives no sense of satisfaction to the one who uses the expression to cover up slipshod work, nor indeed the one who receives it.

Very often the expression becomes, 'It will do for now', intimating that later the task will be improved upon. But how often 'for now,' has a long life, and a temporary job becomes a permanency until, at a crucial moment, a breakdown occurs which can have serious consequences.

Granted, emergencies arise which necessitate immediate action, even though the necessary tools or materials are not available. Then temporary measures become essential. A broken fan belt some miles from the nearest garage on a lonely road leaves you with no option but to contrive some means of continuing your journey, even though you know it will only do temporarily. But it would be foolish indeed if the repair were not made good at the first opportunity.

So the next time you find yourself saying 'It'll do', recognise that you are in danger of adopting a dangerous outlook on life. Determine there and then, if circumstances permit, that you will not allow something inferior to pass, but that what you do will stand up to the severest tests; so that you never have a lurking fear that someone may be seriously inconvenienced if not hurt because you chose to get by.

I know of few expressions more pregnant with future embarrassment than this one. How often that which we have hastily done, not even to our own satisfaction, is unexpectedly recorded on a photograph or comes under the eye of a caller whom we would like to impress favourably. What will he or she think? we ask ourselves, after the visitor has left, knowing that it will not be easy to eradicate the unfavourable impression that has been made. Indeed, we often pay dearly for what could well have been an excusable lapse. The trouble is that the occasional failure to do a good job may become a habit and form the basis for an adverse judgement on our reliability. More important, however, than the effect on others is the fact that we lose self-respect and fail to enjoy the satisfaction that comes from the knowledge of a job well done.

'I'm disappointed in you'

The principal and I were discussing school business in his office. There was a sharp rap on the door. Almost immediately an obviously irate member of staff erupted into the room, sat herself down and delivered herself of the statement: 'I'm disappointed in you.'

From the principal came the calm rejoinder: 'I'm not surprised. I'm often disappointed with myself.'

I did not wait to hear the ensuing conversation, but slipped away quietly.

This happened many years ago. The episode has often come to my mind. I have wondered at the wisdom of the principal's spontaneous response. It is a rare but enviable gift to be able to see and acknowledge our own weaknesses. Yes, we have a quick eye for those of others and, like the good lady quoted above, we may be tempted to express our disappointment with considerable bluntness.

In a way our disappointment is a kind of compliment. At least it gives evidence of having previously had a *fair* opinion of the other person. Our expectations have been reasonably high until some action or lack of action on his or her part causes that esteem to crumble. If we know all the facts we might withhold judgement. But a wider consideration must make us pause. Who can look back over his life and declare never to have caused someone to be disappointed in him?

The fact of the matter is that we should not demand of others what we have not always produced ourselves. We need to recognise that they are subject to the same strains and vexations as cause us not to be on top of things. Troubles seldom come singly. While we are still reeling from that unexpected blow, a second and a third may come in quick succession. In such circumstances how important it is that our friends should be understanding and that we should be also *at such times*.

How privileged are those who know our Lord Jesus. Though aware that our reactions must often have been a cause of disappointment to him, we know that they awoke in him not condemnation but compassion. We need not fear to find him coldly repelling. On the contrary, his grace is poured out more abundantly. And because we are daily learning of him, when disappointed in others we shall have the same response.

And one thing is certain, when the ups and downs of this life end, no one will be disappointed with what Jesus has gone to prepare for us. (John 14:1-3.) Perhaps he is even now putting the last finishing touches to the homes he has commissioned for us. . . .

'I do my own thing'

How would you like to go for a drive with someone who declared, as you stepped into the car, 'I don't care about road signs. I do my own thing'? I think you would get out quicker than you got in, especially if you knew that just down the road you would be joining a main road with a sign warning, 'Give way'.

On life's highway there are some who press ahead regardless – doing their own thing. They are absorbed in the pursuit of their own purposes, giving no thought to the other person. If they continue that way, there may be fatal consequences for them – and possibly for others!

To disregard the signs is suicidal. What signs? The signs that God has erected to protect us from the inevitable fatal crash that will rob us of eternal life.

We may not see the danger involved in disregarding God's laws. To us the way ahead may look attractive and promising. Why worry? But God says, 'Remember the other man's rights.' We may apparently get away with it. Many do for a time. But there is an inescapable penalty attached to selfish action which everyone must ultimately pay.

Even in this life retribution has a way of falling heavily on the heads of those who contravene the laws of decent behaviour. Our newspapers daily record the downfall of even comparatively minor offenders. What happens in this life is nothing to the eternal loss awaiting those who choose to disregard the signs.

How much happier life is for everyone when we learn to give way graciously, to acknowledge that we can't do our own thing. At home, at school, at work, it is so easy to set out on a collision course. At all costs we will have our own way. Unfortunately, other people are involved. They want to exert their own rights, real or imaginary. Just as any sane driver will pause at the warning sign 'Give way', so the Christian will heed the inner warnings of the Word.

 ## 'Thorn in the flesh'

One senses the frustration felt by the apostle Paul because of what he called his 'thorn in the flesh'. In more recent times the poet Milton, writing on his blindness, experienced a similar emotion. Both these men, however, were able to triumph over the limitations which their condition imposed upon them and find assurance that responding in a positive way made their service or apparent lack of it redound to the glory of God.

Most of us, somewhere in life's experience, pass through similar periods of depression at not being able to do what we should like to do. We almost accuse God of shortsightedness in not seeing how much better we could serve him if certain limitations were removed. Jesus had to remind his disciples that, at best, they were unprofitable servants. And we can hardly claim superiority over them!

In many cases frustration acts as a goad to achievement. Finding one avenue of service closed, many have turned their efforts in a different direction and discovered to their delight and amazement a hidden talent which has taken them further in life than the course they originally planned to pursue would have done. To quote a modern example: Joni Eareckson Tada. Prior to the accident that deprived her of physical mobility, she was totally unaware that she had the ability to write inspiring messages which could serve to lift many others out of despondency into the realisation that all was not lost, either in the realm of personal satisfaction or in the power to contribute effectively to the sum of human resilience and achievement.

At this present moment it may seem that there is no light at the end of the tunnel for you. Or, if there is a glimmer of hope, that it can never flood your life with an inner radiance which shines out into other people's lives. Remember it takes but a spark to set alight a great conflagration.

However, in life it is not always the major frustrations which cause us trouble. It is the little things of everyday life which cause the frictions which sour our relationships. Just as grains of sand in otherwise smooth machinery can result in its seizing up, so these little frustrations can bring our peace of mind and self-control to a sudden halt. We need to take stock of the situation before this happens and take appropriate measures. We are all familiar with the oyster's technique, and the resultant beauty which is the delight of so many. Surely if the oyster confronted with a physical problem can do so much, we, with our superior intellect and with divine aid so readily available, can accomplish equally lovely results.

Can it be that our Lord handles with delight the pearls of character that result from a right reaction to our frustrations?

'A man after my own heart'

God's generosity. I'm not thinking about God's bountiful material gifts. Nor the splendours of the eternal home he has promised to his disciples. There is another generosity which is far more moving. It is the generosity of spirit which seizes on the good in others and is silent concerning the bad.

Let me give some examples. I'll start with David. Now we all know how wicked he was: a sure case for God to hold in perpetual contempt. And I'm not just thinking of the Bathsheba episode, though that was shocking enough. Definitely not the man to uphold as a pillar in the church. But listen to God's verdict: 'He's a man after my own heart.'

Obviously there could be no condoning of his faults, but God loved the youth who was so zealous of his honour and so confident of his protection that he dared do what no one else in Israel would venture to do.

Jesus was just like his Father. Who else would have noticed an insignificant little woman casting a mere pittance into the treasury? In his eyes that gift was magnified by love. French writer Maupassant told a similar story of a poor woman who knitted a pair of coarse gaudy socks for the brilliant young doctor who cared for her. He wore them to show his appreciation and, in doing so, revealed a generosity of spirit which moves the reader.

Who can read without appreciation the tribute paid to Daniel by the heavenly being sent to reveal to him the beacon-light of truth which guides us today through the labyrinth of history! 'O Daniel, a man greatly beloved.' (Daniel 10:11.) What a generous greeting that was. How much it revealed of the speaker as well as the one on whose ears the greeting fell.

We are so prone to allow others' mistakes to blot out the transformation that God is operating in their lives. 'You are my friends,' said Jesus. Was it because he was blind to their faults? They were at times quarrelsome and self-seeking, bold and cowardly, faithless and trusting. But Jesus saw the end product of his love and was not ashamed to call them friends.

Some expressions re-echo in our hearts: 'Neither do I condemn you', 'Father, forgive them, they know not what they do', 'You will be with me in paradise', spoken not to saints but to sinners whose actions and words had caused him the deepest distress.

And so it is, as I look upon my fellow worshippers in church, I say to myself, these are the men and women whom Jesus loves. They are those who, in his generosity, he calls his brothers and sisters.

Our attitude should be the same as that of Christ Jesus. (See Philippians 2:5.)

'All I want is my rights'

'I'm not asking for favours. All I want is my rights.' The speaker voiced the sentiments of the little knot of friends gathered around him. They too wanted justice, and who could blame them?

I like the man who is as much concerned for another's rights as his own. In fact, I have known some who were more intent on seeing that others were fairly dealt with than they were on safeguarding their own interests. They recognised that in an imperfect world things do not always work out right and they felt they could take it. But they knew that some people are thrown completely off balance when they have been dealt with unjustly and for them they would put forth strenuous efforts to restore the balance.

It is surely right to champion the weak or the wrongfully accused. Yet we must be careful to know all the facts in a

'All I want is my rights'

case before we take sides. We run the danger of attributing wrong motives and unjust actions to a third party as a result of judging from appearances only, or on the version of an incident which is reported to us from one *side* only. Then we ourselves can be guilty of an injustice.

This is not to say that wrongs do not occur. When they do, we need to keep a sense of proportion and not heap upon ourselves a further evil by allowing ourselves to be robbed of our Christian serenity. So often on such occasions people harbour bitterness in their hearts, become alienated from their brethren, lose their trust in God, at precisely the time when they most desperately need the comfort and guidance of his Spirit. We should always remember that God's love for us has not wavered, nor his desire for us to share eternity with him.

We must be careful not to take it out on God and ourselves in times of distress. The only safe course in life is to determine that, come what may, we will by the grace of God retain our Christian composure and confidence. It is wonderfully reassuring to know that whatever the circumstances there is One who retains his affection for us and has promised to make us more than conquerors if we will let him.

The last thing I want out of the totality of *my* life is justice. *Mercy* is what I need, not justice! King David was quick to react to the prophet Nathan's story of arbitrary action and pronounced immediate sentence, only to find that he had unwittingly condemned himself. This led him to throw himself on God's mercy. We may not have just such a rude awakening, but I venture to say that not one of us will want to stand before the judgement seat of God and claim his deserts rather than God's *clemency*.

How big is your God?

It takes such a little thing to obscure one's vision. Hold a couple of coins close to your eyes and you will blot out a whole landscape, yet how many people focus their attention on gold to the exclusion of all else? They have thought to secure all the other good things of life but have ended it in a spiritual desert.

Saddest of all is the experience of one who allows anything in his life to shut out God. One member of the congregation looms so large in his eyes, because of a mistake, that God is blocked from view. But surely God is bigger than any man or any circumstance?

The fiery furnace was not big enough to hide God from the devoted sight of three young Hebrew civil servants. His brothers' unnatural treatment could not conceal from Joseph the vision of a caring God. Paul's God was too big to be shut out from view by dungeon or sword. Countless Christians through the centuries could still see God as they went to their deaths. Indeed, the Scriptures speak of an innumerable host who never lost sight of God and will awaken to an everlasting welcome.

How is it with you? Does God loom bigger before your eyes than any happening at home, or work, or church? His glory is written on the mountain heights and flowing streams; in lofty forests and flower-studded pastures. The heavens declare the glory of God and the microscope reveals the amazing delicacy of his touch.

Is there anything bigger or better than God? A thousand years may pass; he is still there. Near or far, at your side or a million miles away, he is there.

Can we afford to let little things shut him out? Shall we be like little children with their coins before their eyes declaring there is nothing to be seen? That may be fun for children, but it is not fun for adults. When we shut out God, we shut ourselves out from eternal bliss. Sadly, also, we so easily close the door of eternity on those who depend on us to tell them that nothing can separate us from his love manifested at infinite cost at Calvary.

How big is your God?

Is he just a character in the Bible or is the Bible story an episode in the eternity of his existence? Do we seek to comprehend God in our theology or is all we have learned or imagined but a glimpse of him seen through a glass darkly? Does our science sound the depths of the mysteries of God's creation?

Those who know most know that they have but touched the fringe of knowledge, all of which is everyday stuff to God. He transcends our wildest imaginings and estimates. Yet we shut him out.

Stop. Ask yourself, 'How big is my God?' It will pay you to do so.

'It may come in useful . . .'

'I don't know what we shall do if we ever have to move,' she said. 'My husband holds on to *everything*. You should see our spare room and our garage! They are choc-a-bloc full of rubbish. He always says you never know when a thing may come in handy. The fact is that they do, occasionally, though they usually take a lot of finding.'

But that is not the kind of hoarding that causes me concern. Material things can eventually be dumped if necessary. I'm concerned with the hoarding of memories. Material things are inert. They have no lives of their own. They do not affect their surrounding. But memories, particularly unhappy ones, have a pervasive influence. They colour things. They taint things. They predispose one to anticipate the worst. They poison one's thoughts. They obscure the sun. They embitter relationships.

Take for example that offhand remark passed by one who was your friend twenty years ago. It has been rankling ever since. It has caused you to keep your distance, to hold him or her at arm's length. It ought to have been thrown out of your mind years ago. But it's still there and you've been feeling cold ever since. Indeed, just to see others on friendly terms with him or her puts you off.

The strange thing is that one unpleasant experience so often casts a veil over the many pleasant ones we enjoyed and impoverishes our lives until we have a mental clean-up. It's a kind of intoxication, but with a hangover incomparably more devastating than that resulting from a drinking bout. Many people have learned from one such experience never again to indulge. Unfortunately, hoarded grievances prolong the problem indefinitely and leak their poison into other aspects of our lives.

I hope you will not let pride prevent you from throwing out the accumulated rubbish, so that the sunshine of God's love can flood every corner of your mind, filling you with spiritual health and joy and a sense of well-being.

 ## 'You have to laugh'

What a vast range of responses the word laughter covers. Everything from a subdued titter to a raucous bellow, from appreciation to scorn and contempt, from encouragement to derision.

The difference in nature is determined by two little words, *with* and *at*. To laugh *with* someone is to enter into that person's happiness. To laugh *at* is to underline another's discomfiture That is speaking in general terms. To laugh *with* may indicate complicity, while to laugh *at* may be a sign of

'You have to laugh'

fortitude. Perhaps we should consider a number of situations and determine, if we can, the appropriateness of the resultant laughter.

Let us think first of the laughter of sheer joy. How infectious it is! How it dispels the gloom and sends us on our way with lighter foot and brighter outlook. It has in it no malice, but is like the babbling of a brook sparkling in the glowing sunshine.

I well remember the first orchestral concert I attended. I had great difficulty in suppressing the laughter of sheer enjoyment which threatened to burst forth. I've never quite got over that early enthusiasm, which makes me a dangerous companion for anyone with a sense of decorum. What would people think if I actually laughed aloud for pleasure? It's unthinkable!

People do laugh in concerts and I do blush for them as they respond to the sullied innuendos of the so-called entertainer who would daub slime on the purest lily and think he was being funny.

The laughter I like best is that which reveals participation in another's happiness. Such was the laughter to which Sarah referred, when she said that at the news of the birth of her son Isaac everybody would laugh with her. Contrast that with the scornful laughter of the soldiers who mocked Jesus' claim to be a King, or that of the priests who stood around the cross and derided our Lord in his agony because he was assured of his divine Sonship. The laughter of participation in another's joy will echo throughout eternity. The laughter of scorn will die with its perpetrator.

I mentioned the laughter of fortitude. It is akin to the ability to see the funny side of an otherwise unfortunate situation. It will often relieve tension and so begin recovery from hurt. Your laughter may remove your hostess's embarrassment over a mishap, particularly if you were the victim of it.

There is an old saying: 'Laugh and the world laughs with you; weep and you weep alone.' But it must not be assumed that tears alone denote participation in another's feelings. Overflowing into laughter can add greatly to another's happiness in success. So let us learn to laugh with those who have cause for rejoicing.

'A cheerful heart is good medicine, but a crushed spirit dries up the bones.' (Proverbs 17:22.)

'I know a short cut...'

'Welcome! We expected you a long time ago.'

'Oh, we thought we would take a short cut and somehow missed our way. But we're here at last,' our visitors replied.

Which set me thinking on the subject of short cuts. I remembered a short cut we had taken in Rwanda which resulted in our spending the night in an upside-down car suspended over a mountain torrent. We did eventually arrive home about noon the next day, instead of around six the previous evening, an episode in which God's protecting hand was very evident.

But it is not the physical short cuts that present the greatest risks. Indeed, nature teaches us that mighty oaks do not reach their height and girth by sudden spurts. True, some seasons are productive of greater growth than others. But

'I know a short cut ...'

every successive year adds to their ultimately impressive size.

Knowledge and the wisdom to use it well require steady systematic application. Scholastic achievement cannot be cheaply attained, though a title may be bought in some places. Here there is no short cut. It takes but a little while to discover the difference between a true scholar and the one whose academic prowess is only a veneer. In the latter case one is soon disillusioned, whereas continued contact with a true scholar is as rewarding as deep-mining in search of precious metals.

This is true in many walks of life. Strength of character develops through a life of faith. Though here, thank God, time is not the important factor, but faith The youth who lives close to God will have a strength that others do not acquire in a lifetime. The fact is that the young may ally themselves to the infinite wisdom of God. Witness Joseph, Jeremiah, Daniel and the Lord Jesus himself. The totality of consecration, not time, is the determining factor here.

Spiritual giants are to be found among the youth of today and such *will* do and indeed *do* do exploits. Such recognise that their strength is in God and give proof of an endearing modesty. These do not seek for position and office. To do so is very dangerous. To shoulder responsibilities for which one is not fitted is to run the risk of disaster to oneself and the cause one is appointed to serve.

A prime example of the evil consequences of taking short cuts is seen in the collapse of edifices where a disregard for sound workmanship and tested materials has taken place. Appearances may have been excellent, but unexpected stress has resulted in collapse.

So it is in our individual lives. We need to build solidly according to the established principles of the Word of God. Then we need not fear the strains of life, the temptations inherent in access to funds, in authority and public acclaim.

Walking on stilts

It was great fun. Finding a couple of lengths of pole, nailing a block of wood on each for foot-rests and then stomping around the garden and viewing the world from a new height.

Actually we were not all that much taller, but we certainly *felt* we were.

However, it didn't take much to make us topple. Indeed, it was part of the fun to see who could stay up the longest in spite of the nudges.

Of course, the glee produced by being six or twelve inches higher did not last long. It was one of childhood's seasonal pastimes, like tops, marbles and conkers. But none of these produced the same temporary sense of superiority.

Most of us abandoned stilts as we grew older, apart from exceptional circumstances, and were content with our natural height. I am not sure, however, that we have all outgrown the stilt *mentality*. . . .

Do we not enjoy standing a bit higher than others? The stilts of pride come in all sorts of shapes and sizes. The house or the street we live in, the social circles in which we move, the size of our bank account, even the clothes we wear and the make of car we drive, all give us that boost which produces a glow of satisfaction.

When these things lift us up in our self-esteem a bit above our neighbours, it is easy to forget that it is only an artificial superiority that they confer. They have not changed our essential selves. It takes only a bump or a slip to reduce us to the common level.

With Christian maturity we learn to evaluate ourselves and others not by reason of the props which make us look taller than we really are. We accept the apostle's admonition not to think of ourselves more highly than we ought to. We see ourselves without the stilts.

There is a legitimate and desirable increase in stature, a growing in grace and knowledge. Without these we remain stunted and deformed.

As I observe the young people these days, I see that generally speaking they are taller than my generation were. Then have benefited from their parents' better understanding of the factors involved in physical growth. Their educational opportunities are greater. These are all grounds for satisfaction. There is also a growing awareness of the needs of others. And one reads with pride of the devoted efforts of many to be of help to their fellows both at home and abroad.

There exists, nevertheless, a danger that material advancement may become the goal of some, that they will feel that the possession of wealth will lift them above others.

Senior members of society and of the congregation look with admiration and approval on their achievements, but pray that they will not lose 'the common touch', to use Kipling's expression. It is good to remember that these things are only stilts and do not really add to a man's stature.

 ## Lighting-up time

Shadows do not exist in darkness. Where there is no light there is no shadow. Go out on a sunlit day and the street, which on a dull day is evenly lit, will show contrasting areas of light and dark. But the shadows cast by the houses with their backs to the sun are nevertheless not so deep as on sunless days, for the surrounding brightness actually relieves the darkness of the shadow while seeming to accentuate it. If you make use of a light meter you will quickly verify this fact. The reverse is also true. The electric torch which gives such a bright light at nighttime makes a barely perceptible difference when shone in the sunlight. It can dazzle when

Lighting-up time

darkness falls, but not when shone under radiant skies.

Many feel that they have only a very small contribution to make as members of large congregations. Their fellows are so much more talented. They can add so little, they think, to the general brightness. But let them join a small community or congregation and they will shine effectively. I'm not speaking of shining for self-glory, but of humble, joyful service which will not be lost as it might be amid the crowd.

We need to maximise our light source by moving into the dark areas where light does not penetrate. When World War I began, Foreign Secretary Sir Edward Grey said: 'The lights are going out all over Europe. I shall not see them lit again in my lifetime.' It would be wonderful if our Lord, reversing this picture, could say with joy: 'I see the lights going on all over the world.' A torch is much more useful in the dark than is an extra light in a room already ablaze with lights.

What is there to be said about the shadows? Do they have anything to contribute? The same road which lures us to the sunny side in winter provides us with welcome relief when the blazing summer sun saps our energies.

On many occasions I travelled hundreds of miles through treeless areas in Africa. 'We'll pull up for lunch at the next shade-giving tree,' we used to promise ourselves. But we would have to wait five, ten, fifteen minutes, perhaps half an hour, before we found even scanty shade. In life the sunless days also have their role to play in our journey heavenward. But even on those days the darkness is alleviated by the glow that the knowledge of God's love reflects into it. In any case, darkness and light are both alike to him.

Yes, shadows are illusory when they make us think that we are really in a deplorably dark spot in our experience. They can come only when the glorious sun is shining. When things are dark we can be sure God will bring us out into the sunshine of his love, for he knows that light and dark alike have their place in the development of a character which will not look shabby in the glorious light of our heavenly home.

'Among friends'

The story of David and Jonathan is a favourite one with me. Neither sought the other's friendship for personal advantage. Indeed, for Jonathan it meant the loss of a throne to which he might have thought he had a legitimate claim. In David's case the friendship outlived his friend's death and manifested itself in the care he took of Jonathan's crippled son.

Such friendships enrich one's life. From personal experience I can testify to the enduring character of friendships formed in college days, friendships which have lasted for over sixty years and which are as vivid after many years of separation as when they were first formed. Mine were in several cases formed abroad so that I have not been able to think of, for example, Germans and Italians as enemies – and could not, even during the stressful years of war.

The last of those foreign friends died recently, but how rich and inspiring are the memories and how much they add to the anticipated joy of reunion when our Lord returns.

Such friendships call for giving as well as receiving. I do not mean material gifts. They have no part in the bonds which unite real friends. We do well to cultivate such friendships when we are young. In my experience those formed during college days are most worthwhile. They create a pattern of responsiveness which makes it easier for us to open our hearts to people, even when we are older, not fearing the possible betrayal of such friendships in later years.

That's what I find so wonderful about our Lord Jesus. He bestowed his love on those who would betray him, such as Judas, and on those who would oppose him, as did Saul in his Pharisaic blindness. But in many cases it resulted in friendships that endured through many trials, even through death itself.

Even in their absence, loved friends add an invaluable dimension to life. The qualities which we have observed in our friends continue to serve as a challenge and inspiration to us. In some, spirituality breaks the chill of our own indifference. What rebukes our pride is to see others care for their fellows and show an appreciation of their qualities. In still others we find a generosity of spirit.

These good friends prime the light which God wants us to be in this world. Is that going to be part of the glory of heaven – the gathering together in one vast jubilant throng of all the little lights God has used to lighten this present dark world?

 ## He is my brother

The older brother appears only towards the end of the story Jesus told. The younger brother has centre stage in the story of the wealthy farmer. It was the younger brother who chose to leave home to live in the fast lane. His eventual decision to return and the amazing welcome he received from his father have brought hope to generations of prodigals. But my concern is with the older brother. Listen to him.

'What's going on?' he questions as he returns home from the fields. 'What's the meaning of this revelry?' 'Your brother has come home and your father is so glad he is putting on a

He is my brother

feast for him,' reports the servant he questions. At that the elder brother's face darkens. With a scowl he declares, in spite of his father's entreaties, that he will not join in the welcome. Repudiating his own relationship to the returned wanderer, he reproaches his father for showing such favour to the spendthrift. He, who has worked so hard all the time, has never had a party thrown for him, he states. No, he will have no part in the welcome!

Obviously there is no love in his heart for his younger brother. There is no hint in the story that he ever tried to persuade his brother not to go away. Nor did he ever suggest to his father that he himself should leave the comforts of home to go in search of his brother to persuade him to come back.

It was at this point in my meditation on what might have been, that the wonderful compassion of *my* elder Brother almost overwhelmed me.

Jesus dwelt in the glory of his Father's home. He was revered by angel hosts and rejoiced in the companionship of God his Father. But, sensing his brother's hopeless condition, he proposed to go into the far country that was then the home of the prodigal to seek to win him over and bring him back to the family home. Father and Son talked it over. The project was fraught with dangers. What kind of a reception would he have? The angels were filled with dismay. 'You know how bitterly Satan hates you. Now you propose to make yourself vulnerable. And you say you will go as a helpless baby. You won't meet with gratitude. In all probability it will cost you your life.'

But all these protestations could not quench the determined love of their Lord.

In the event their worst fears were justified. He was despised and rejected. He did suffer death at the hands of the one who had gone astray. But hear him as he declares: 'Father, I will that the prodigals shall be with me where I am. Indeed, they shall be joint heirs with me. I'll prepare a home for them beyond their wildest hopes. I'll not have them feeling out of place at the great reception I'll lay on for them. I'll clothe them with my own glorious vesture of righteousness and place a crown on their heads.'

What a brother! Have you received his invitation to the feast? Have you accepted it? Are you making it your priority to be there?

'Many are cold . . . ?'

I got to thinking about how easy it is for us to cheat ourselves. The thought struck after a conversation with a dear member of the congregation which I attend. She commented on the fact that she had always looked upon one member of the congregation as being cold and reserved. Yet when she was ill it was this member who wrote her the kindest and most cheering letters. She realised that she had allowed certain impressions to dominate her thinking with respect to that person and so had deprived herself of a friendship which was very desirable.

I began to wonder how many more of us are in the same position. I know there must be a number because, from time to time, I hear complaints about the coldness of a particular congregation. It is not the heating system that is at fault. Even if it is the coldness of relationships, it can be perceived, but on the basis of misunderstandings. We need to cultivate the habit of believing others are friendly instead of assuming they are not.

Very often others are as shy as we are. They are afraid to speak lest their overtures should be unwelcome. But that is very seldom the case. How *many* times I have heard comments such as: 'I never knew how nice a person he or she was.' I think this happens all too often in the case of the young and the old. Those of us who are getting on in years tend to assume that young people are too full of themselves

'Many are cold . . .?'

and those of their own age to have any time for senior members. The reverse is also true, but how often, once the first step is taken, one finds the young are really caring, and even the old are not petrified in frigidity.

Really the best thing to do is to take it for granted that those around us want to be friendly. When we do this the sun of friendship breaks through, and we rejoice in its warmth.

This has been my experience and I should be a false witness if I failed to say so. So join me in not allowing wrong impressions to cloud our outlook. As a result our congregations everywhere will soon have such a glow of warmth in them that none will be able to say, 'I did not feel welcome', and young and old alike will look forward eagerly to their time of worship which they spend in the company of their fellow believers.